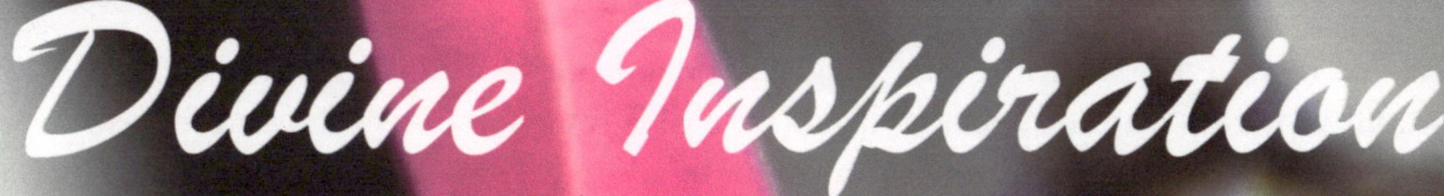

Text from

The New King James Version

of

The Holy Bible

Photography by

Rudolph Valentino Wiggins

11.951 845154LV00009B/149 [430096098]

Divine Inspiration

Manufactured in the United States of America.

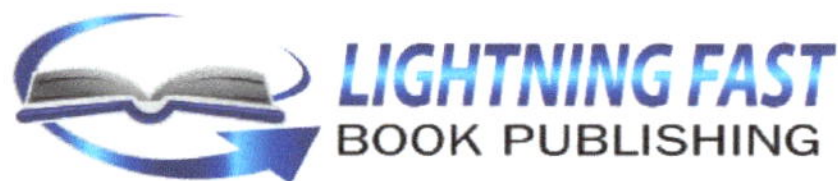

www.lfbookpublishing.com

Summary: Original photography coupled with divine spiritual messages to inspire the reader.

ISBN: 978-0-9994653-8-7

Table of Contents

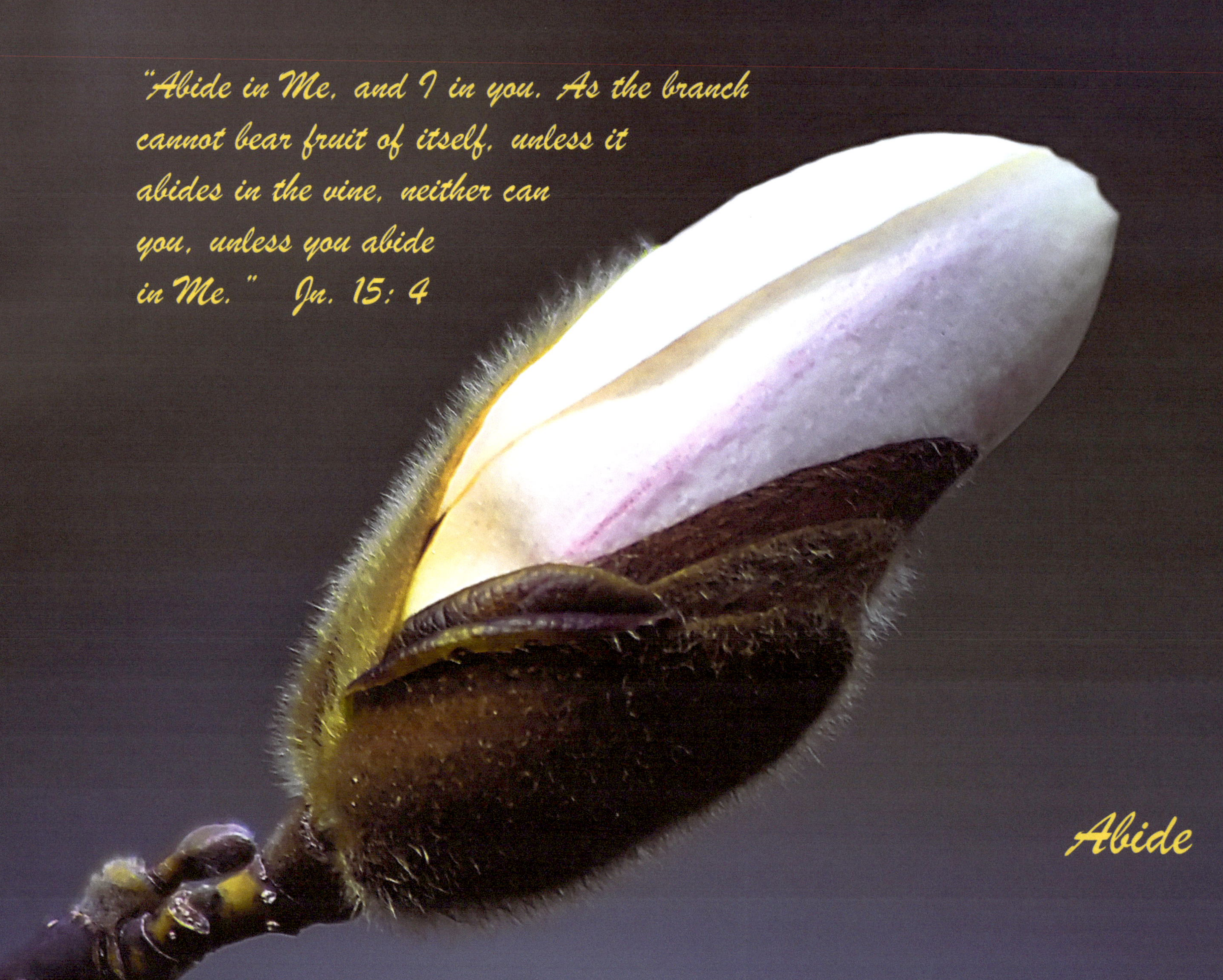
"Abide in Me, and I in you. As the branch
cannot bear fruit of itself, unless it
abides in the vine, neither can
you, unless you abide
in Me." Jn. 15: 4
Abide

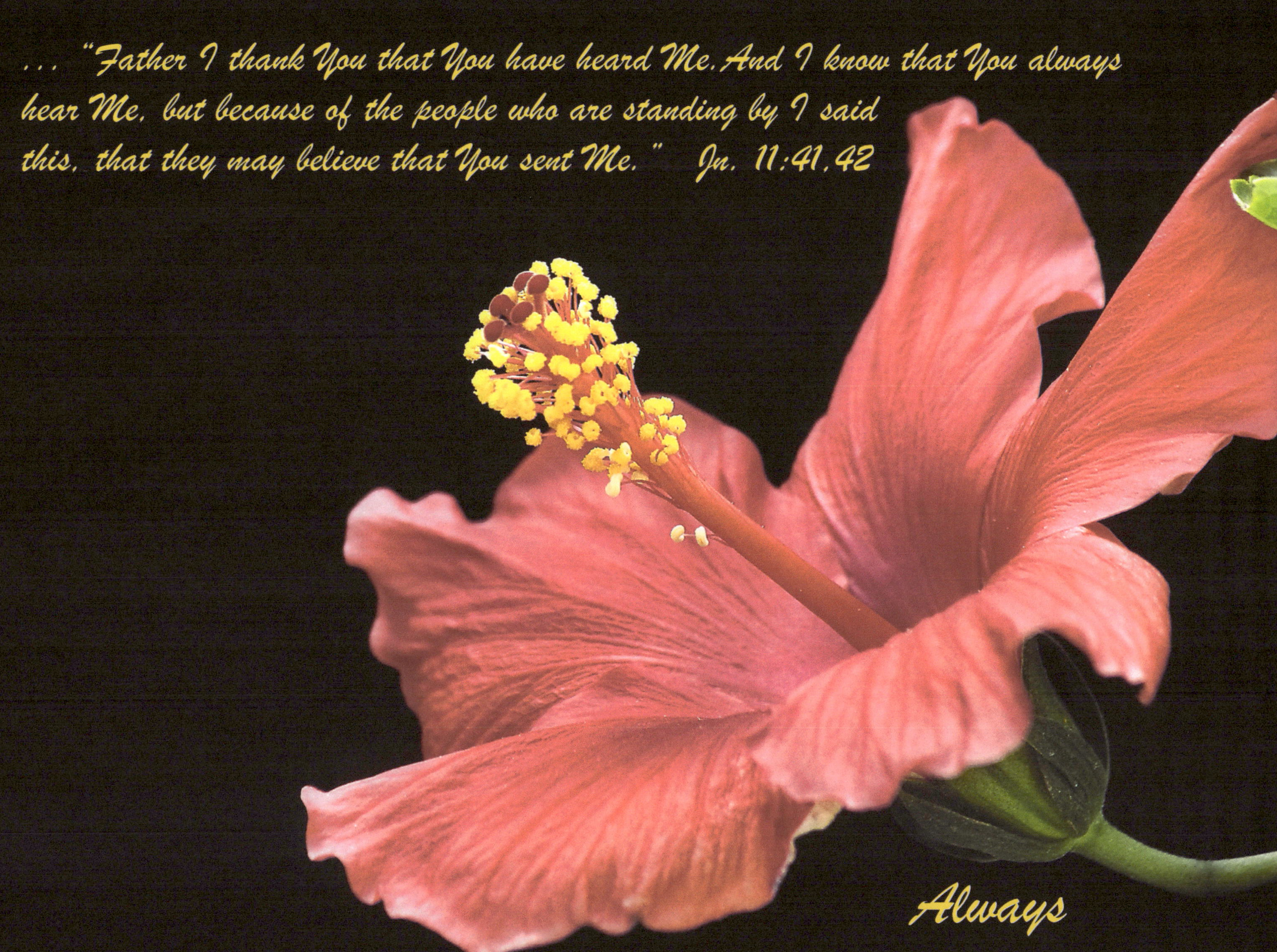
. . . "Father I thank You that You have heard Me. And I know that You always
hear Me, but because of the people who are standing by I said
this, that they may believe that You sent Me." Jn. 11:41, 42
Always

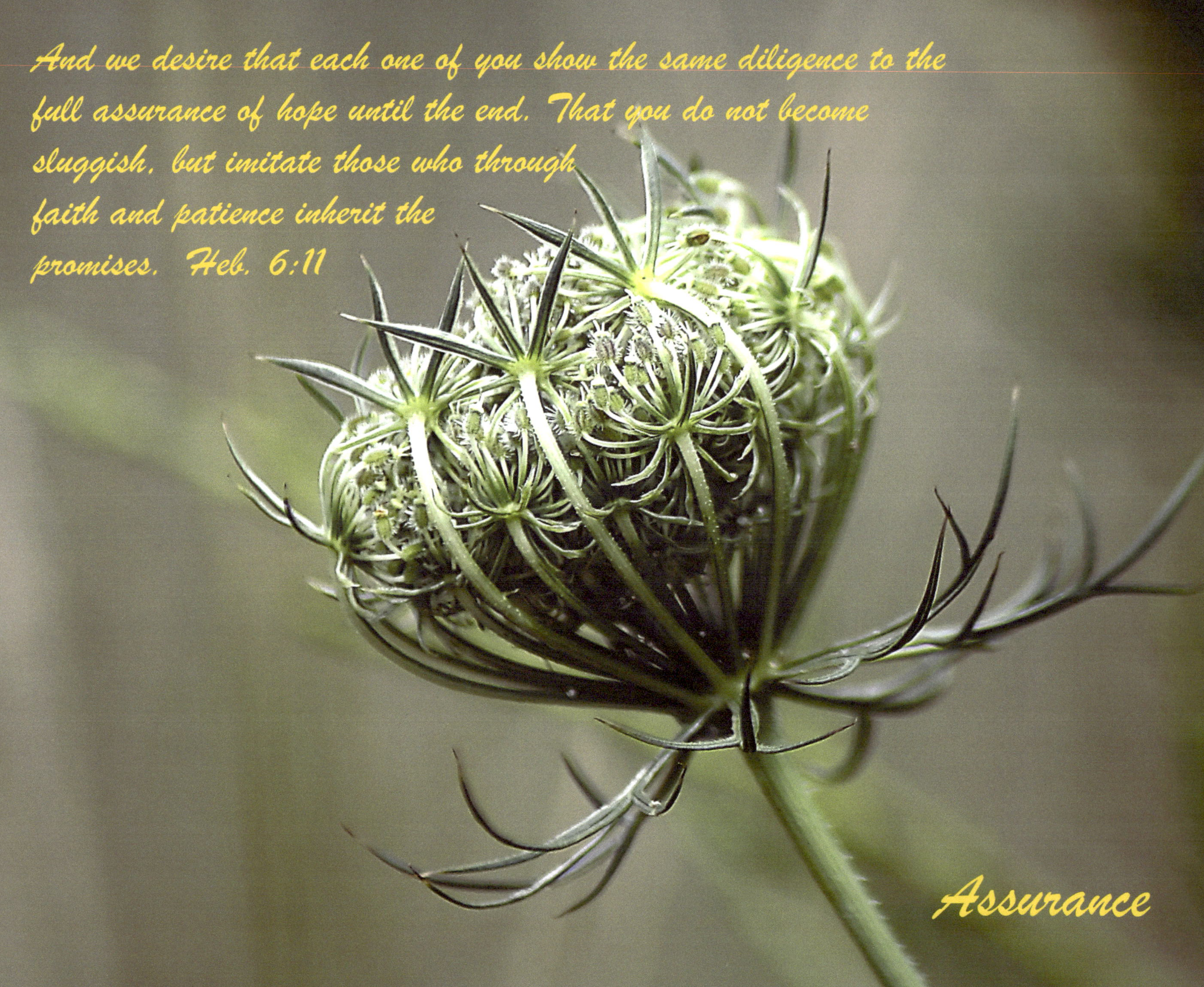
And we desire that each one of you show the same diligence to the
full assurance of hope until the end. That you do not become
sluggish, but imitate those who through
faith and patience inherit the
promises. Heb. 6:11
Assurance

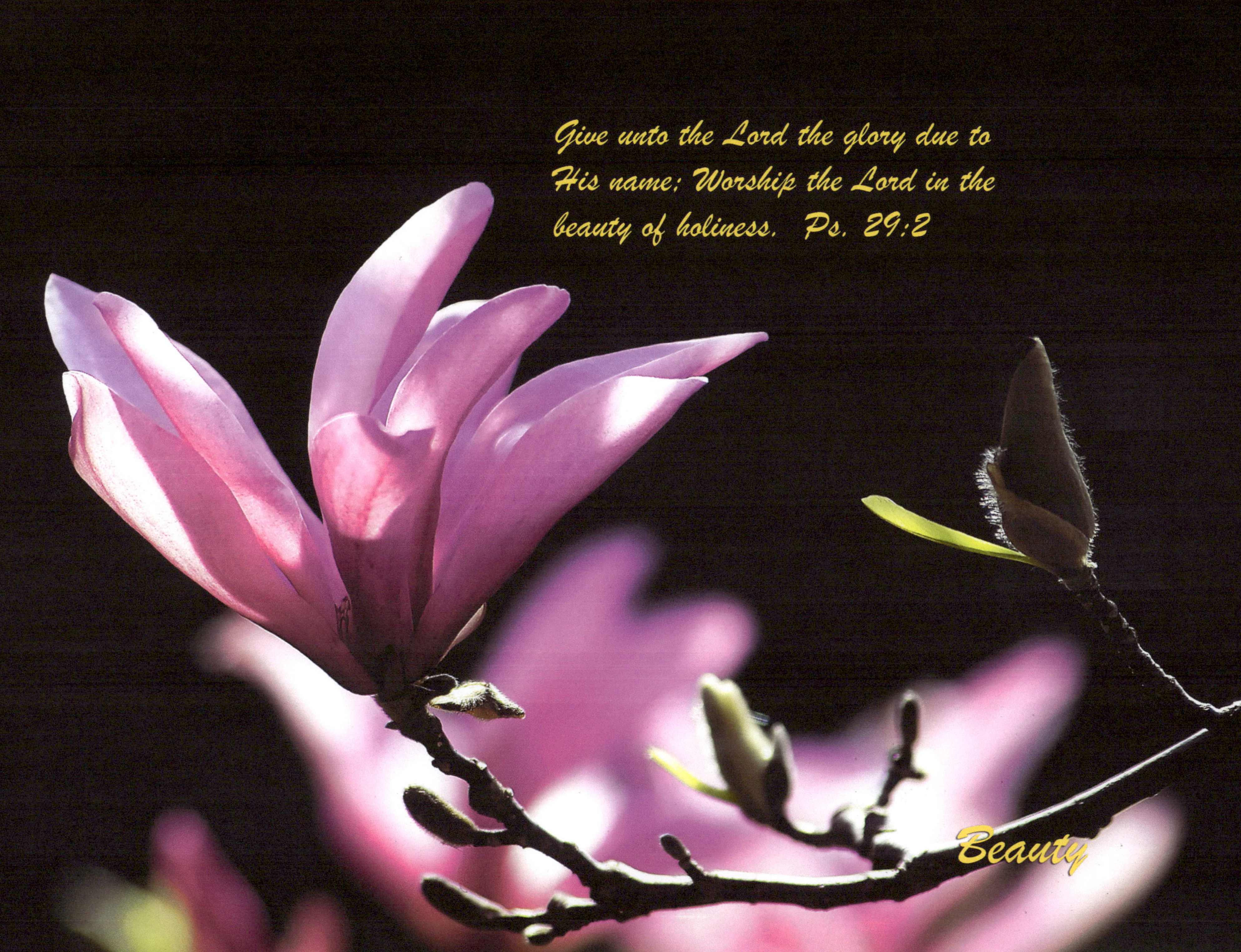
Give unto the Lord the glory due to
His name; Worship the Lord in the
beauty of holiness. Ps. 29:2
Beauty

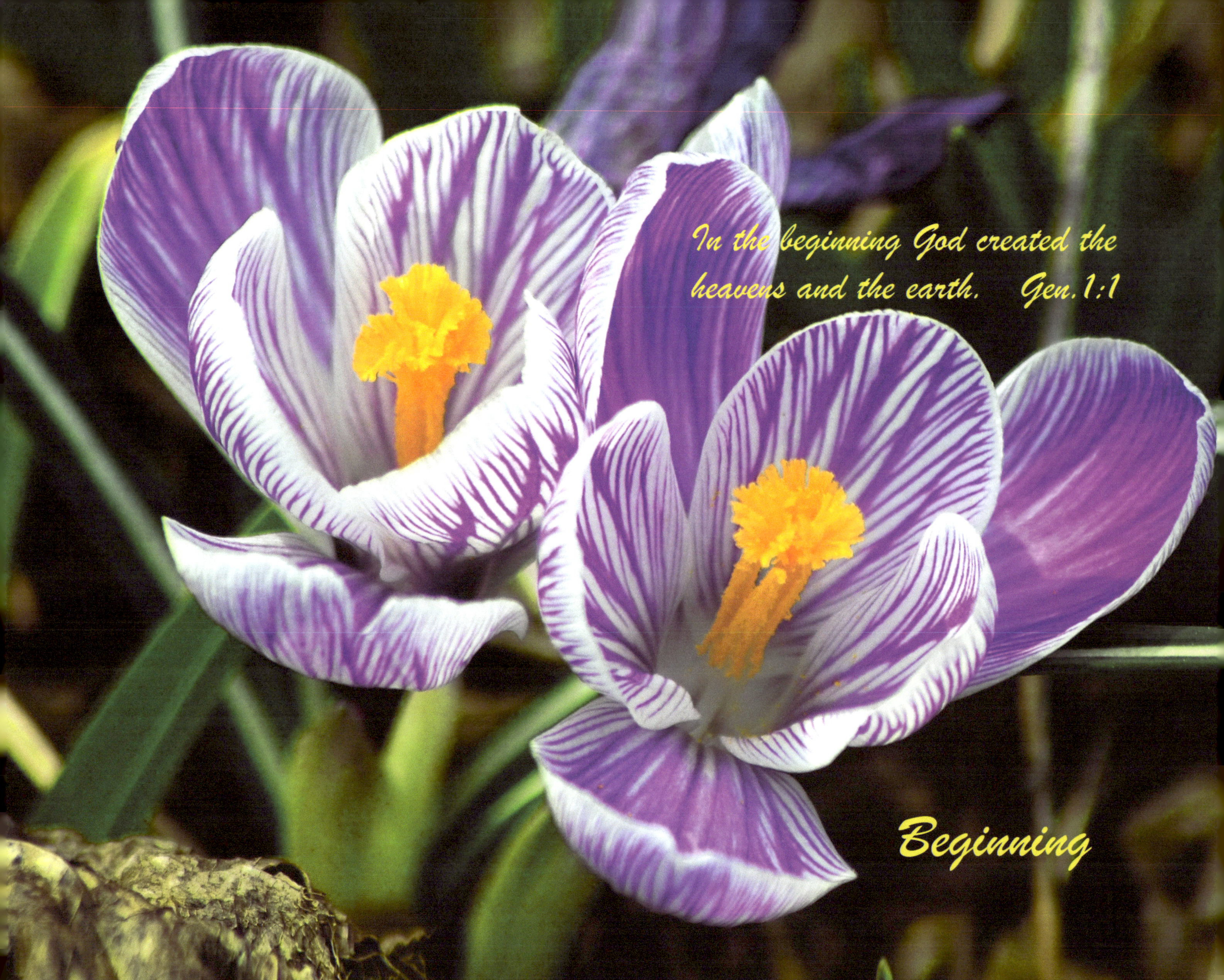
In the beginning God created the
heavens and the earth. Gen. 1:1
Beginning

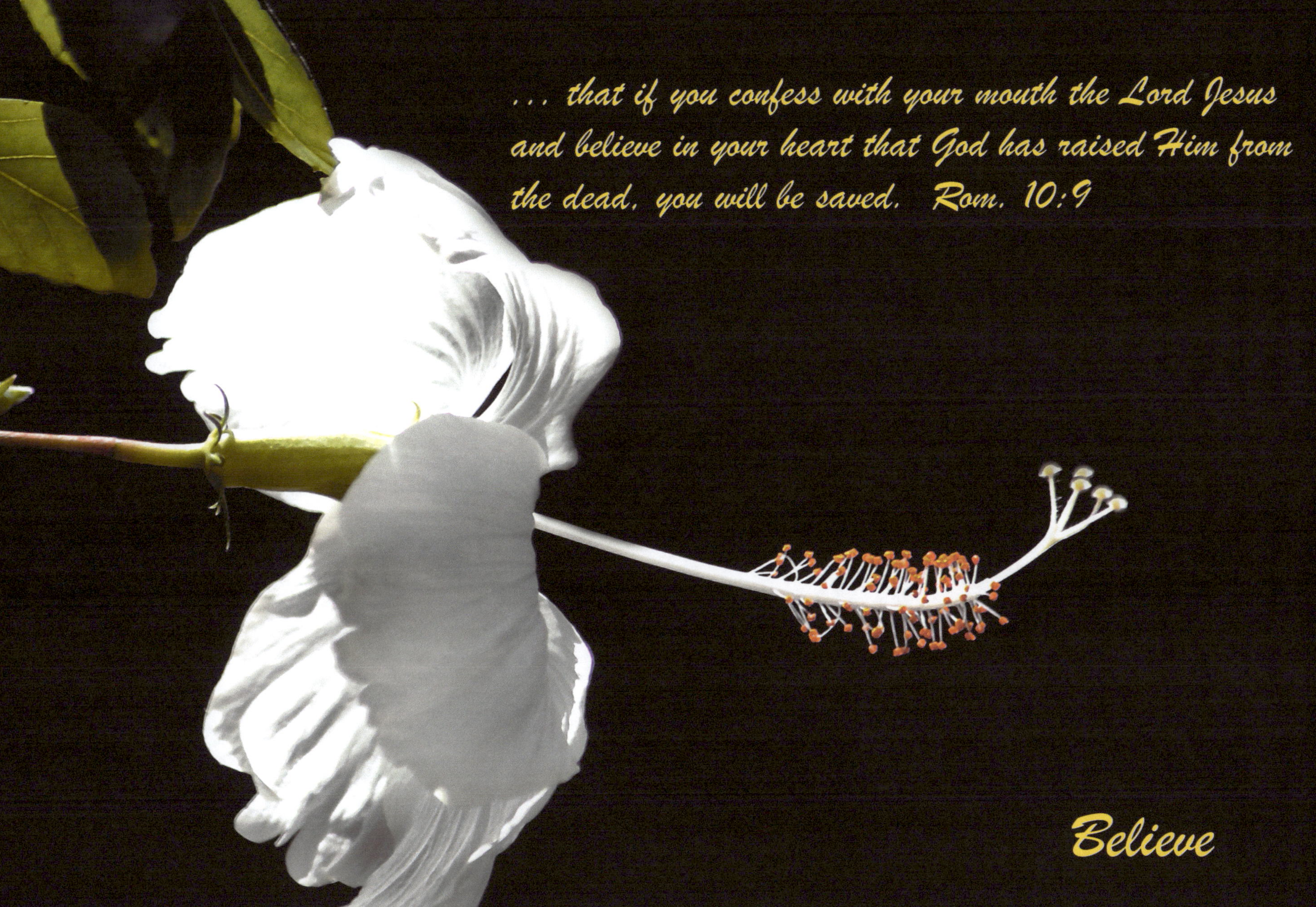
… that if you confess with your mouth the Lord Jesus and believe in your heart that God has raised Him from the dead, you will be saved. Rom. 10:9
Believe

Blessed are the poor in spirit, for theirs is the kingdom of heaven. Mt. 5:3

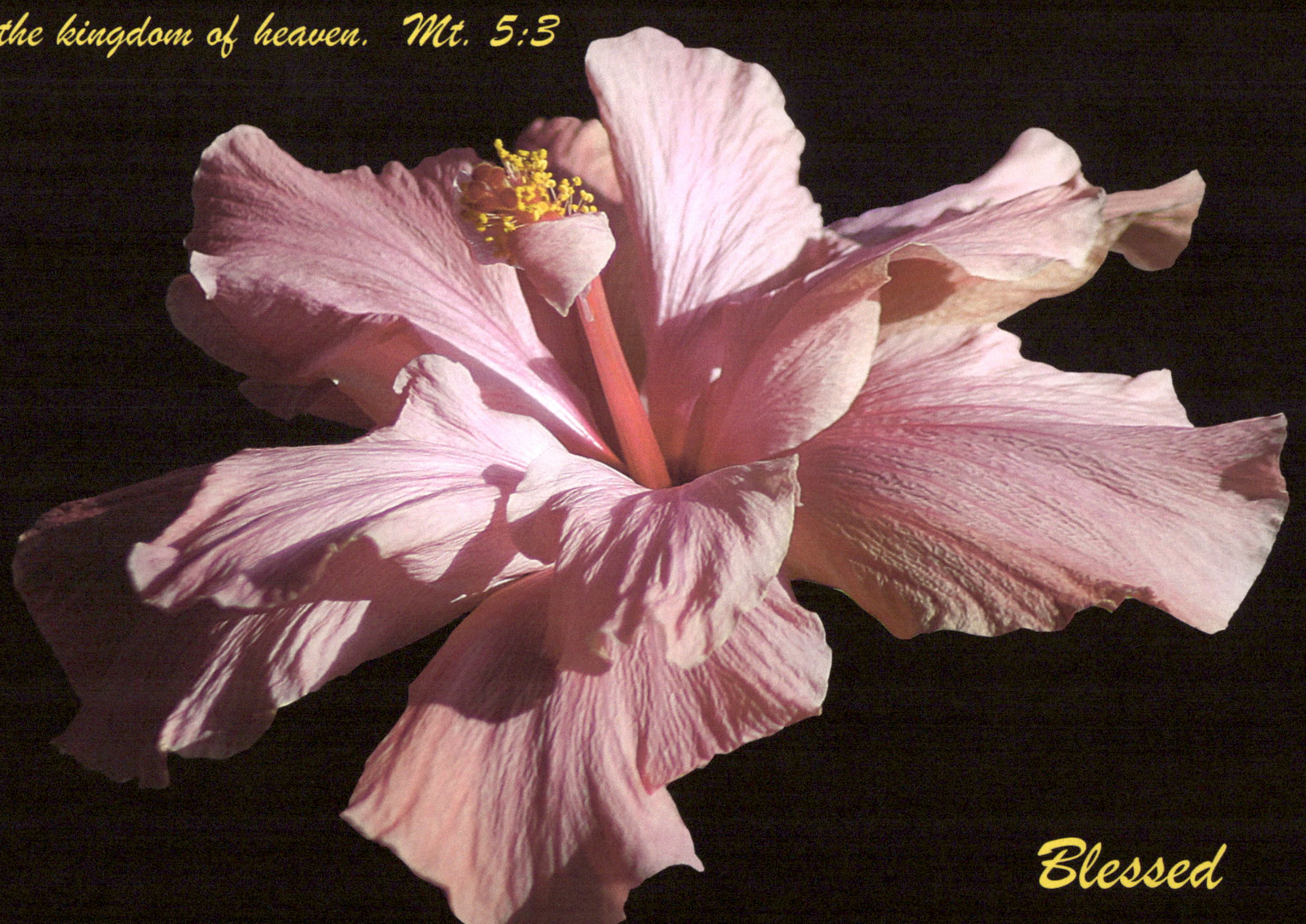

Blessed

But above all these things put on love,
which is the bond of perfection. Col. 3:14

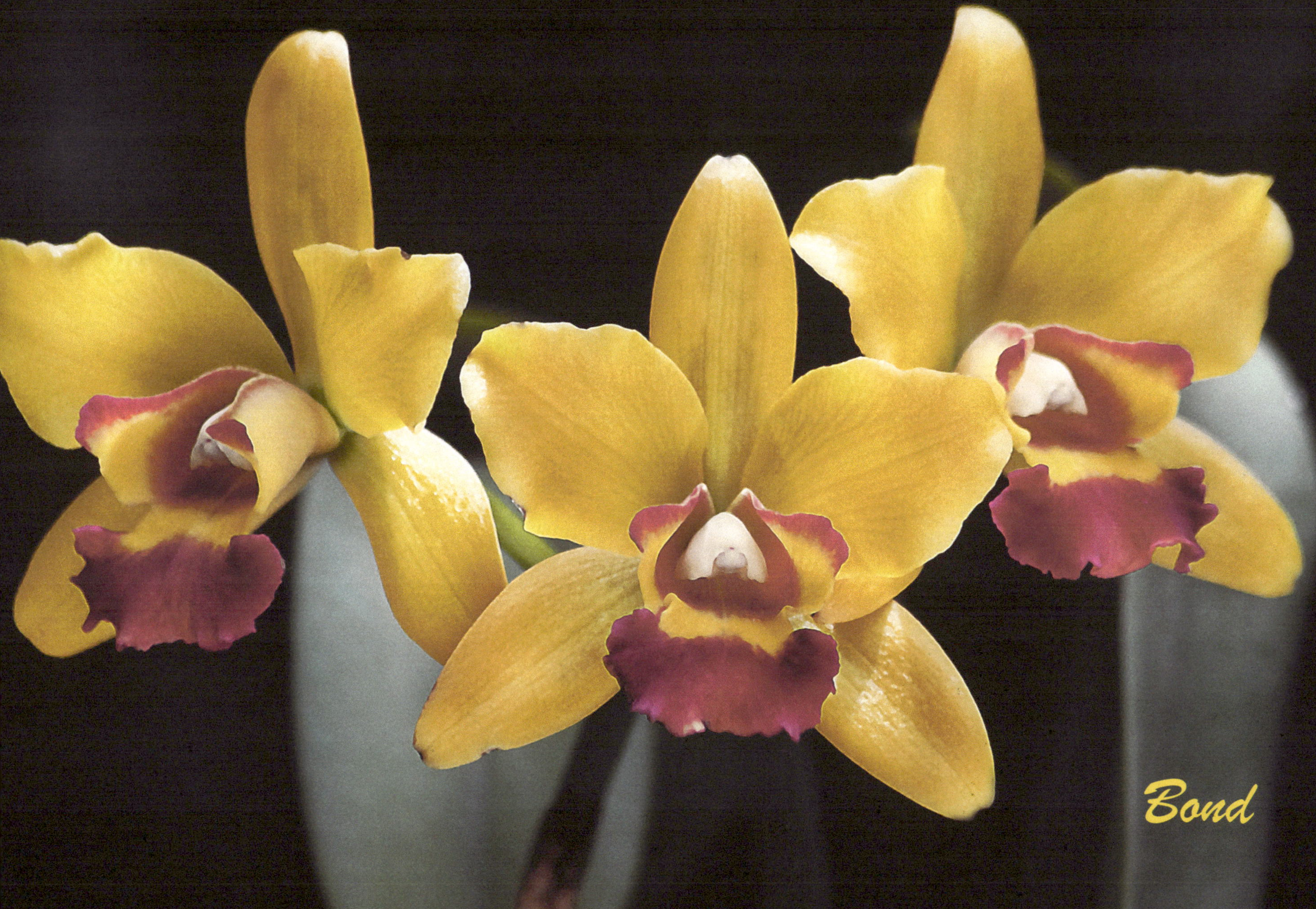

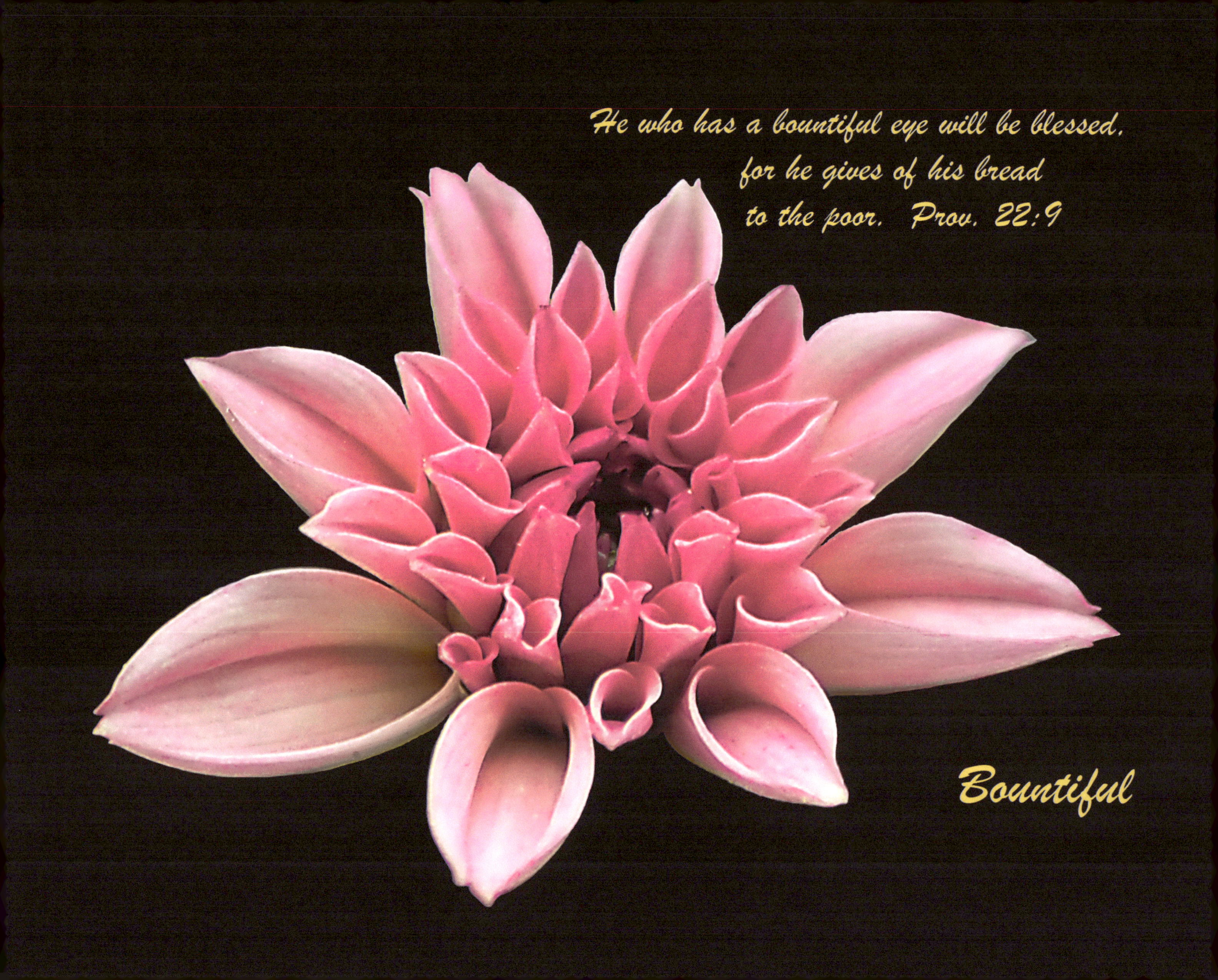

He who has a bountiful eye will be blessed,
for he gives of his bread
to the poor. Prov. 22:9

Bountiful

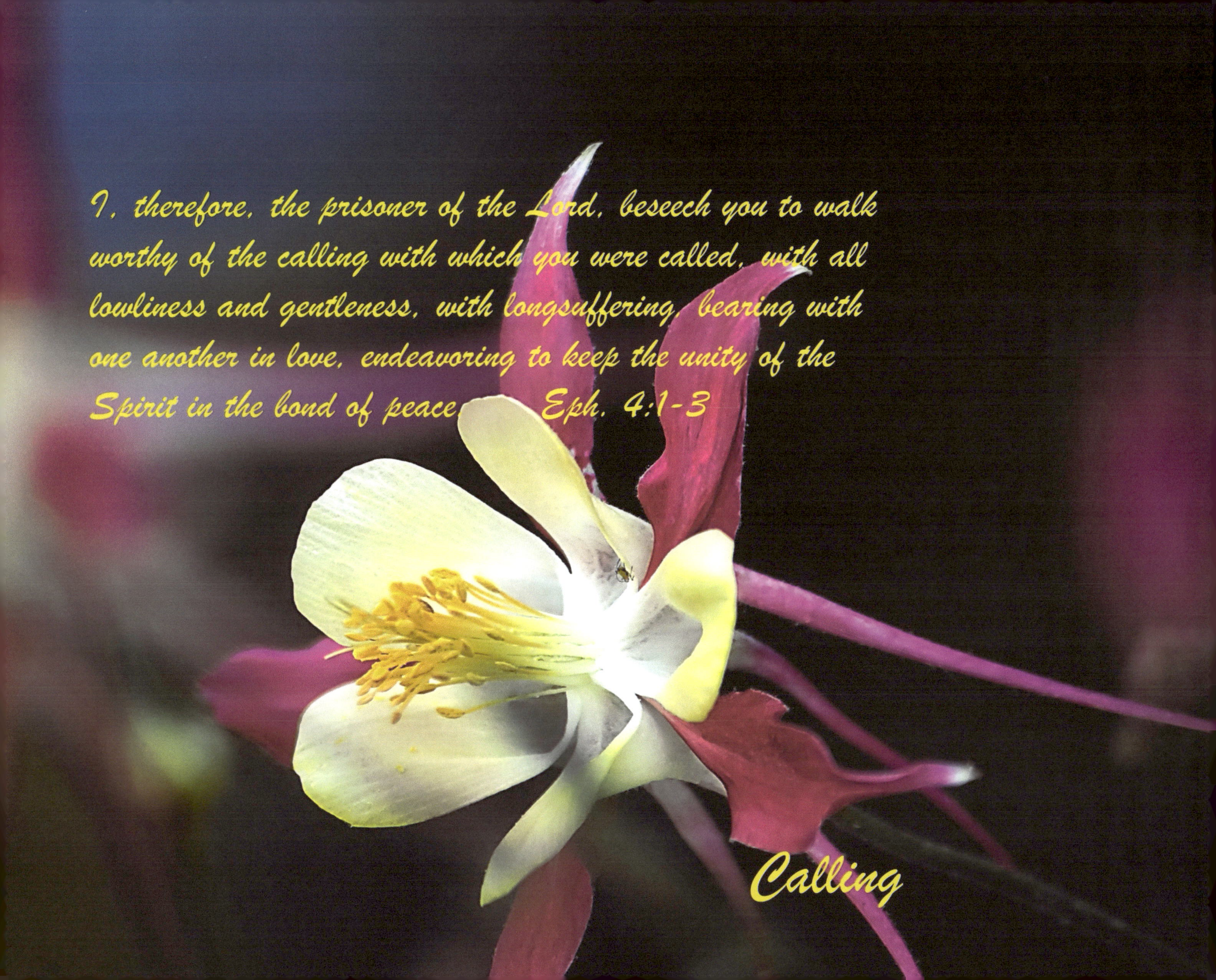

I, therefore, the prisoner of the Lord, beseech you to walk
worthy of the calling with which you were called, with all
lowliness and gentleness, with longsuffering, bearing with
one another in love, endeavoring to keep the unity of the
Spirit in the bond of peace. Eph. 4:1-3

Calling

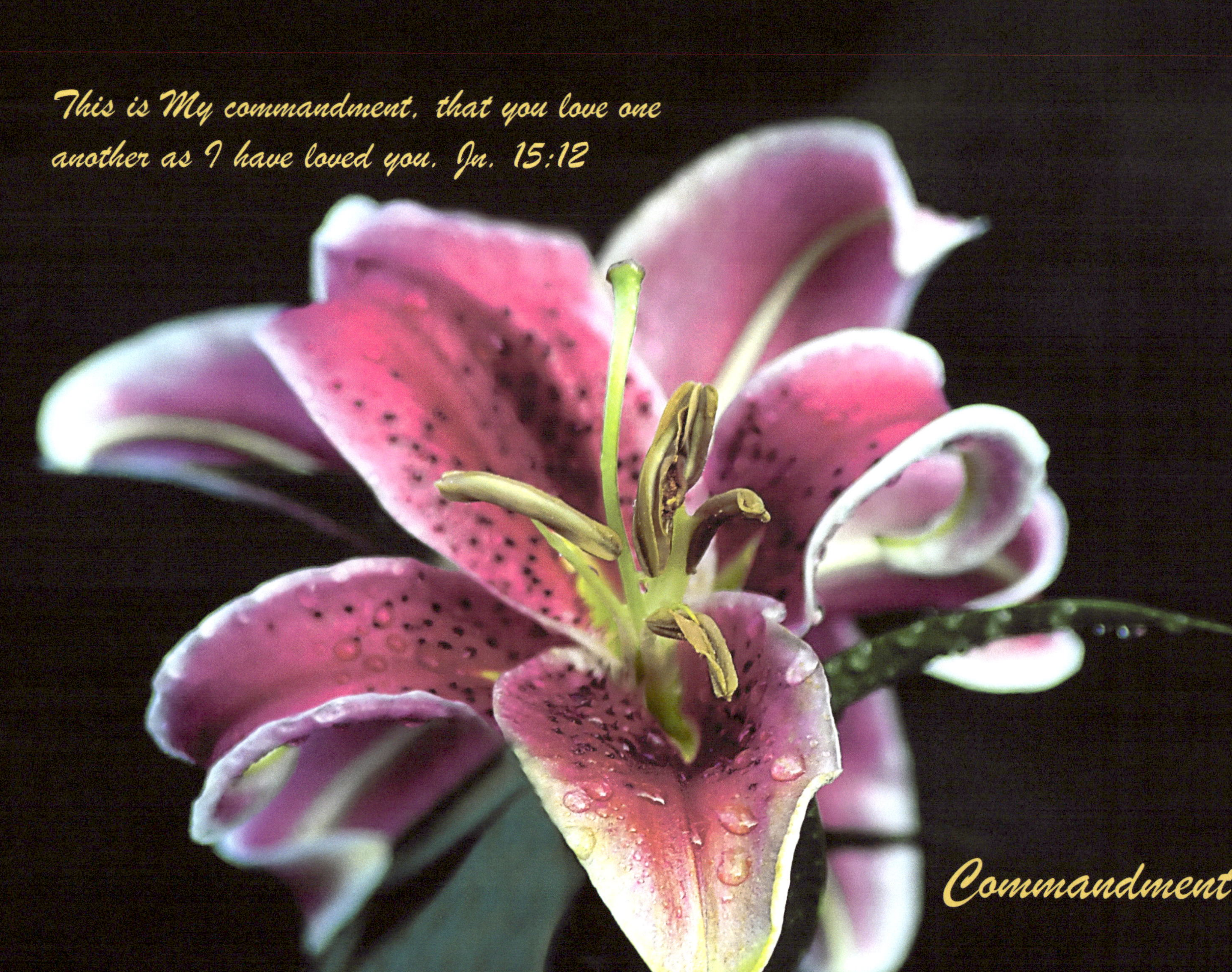
This is My commandment, that you love one
another as I have loved you. Jn. 15:12
Commandment

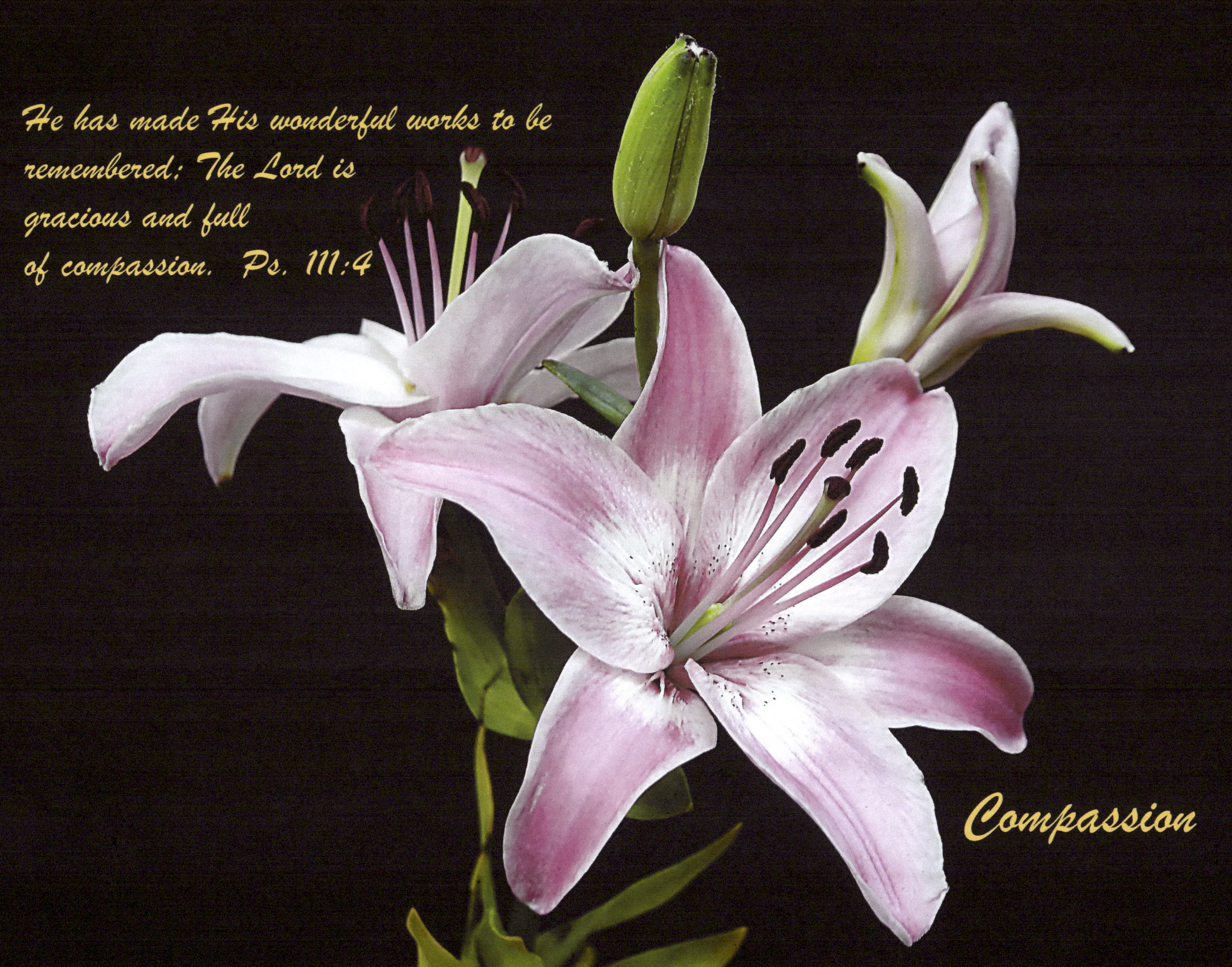
He has made His wonderful works to be
remembered; The Lord is
gracious and full
of compassion. Ps. 111:4
Compassion

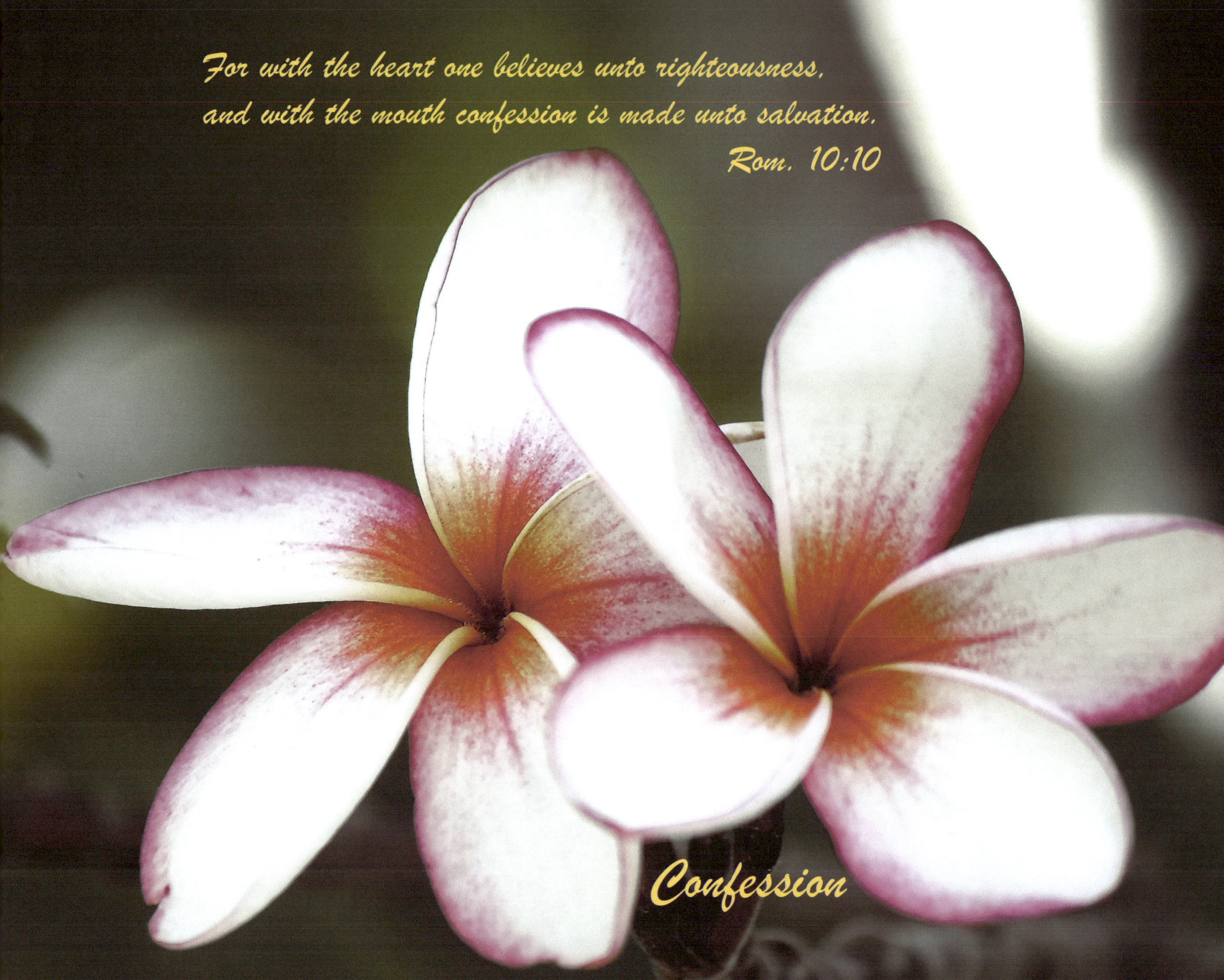
For with the heart one believes unto righteousness,
and with the mouth confession is made unto salvation.
Rom. 10:10
Confession

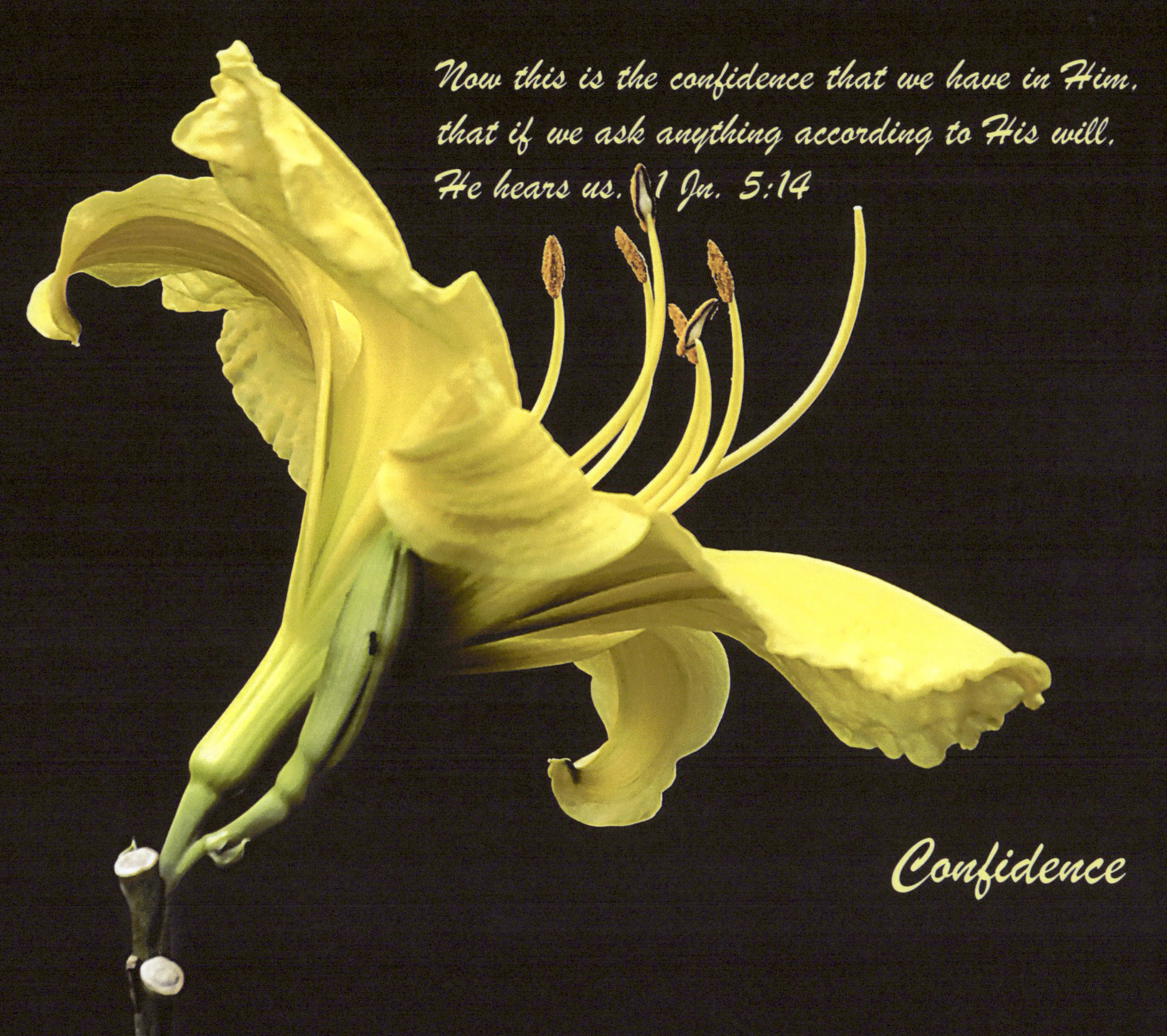
Now this is the confidence that we have in Him,
that if we ask anything according to His will,
He hears us. 1 Jn. 5:14
Confidence

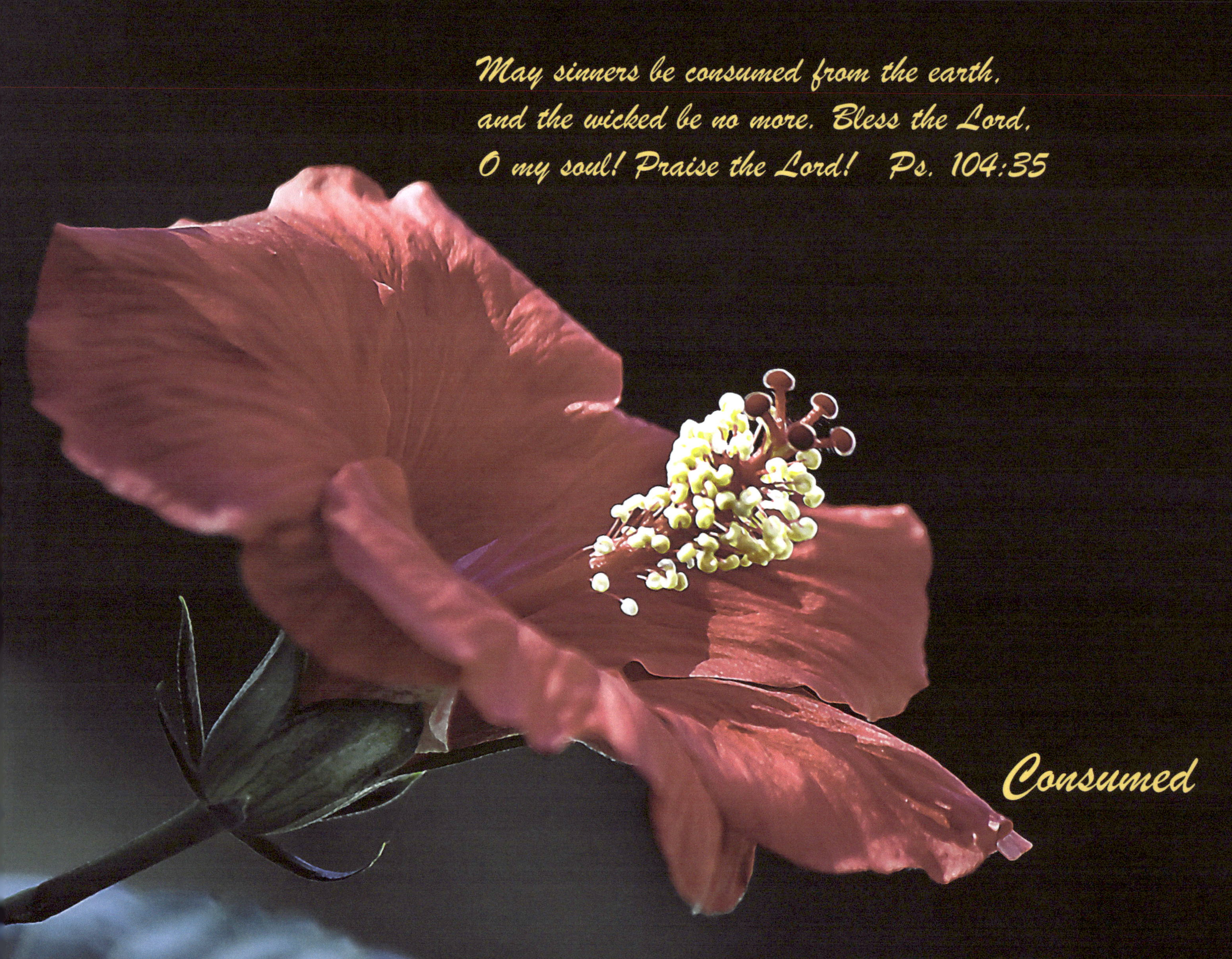
May sinners be consumed from the earth,
and the wicked be no more. Bless the Lord,
O my soul! Praise the Lord!   Ps. 104:35
Consumed

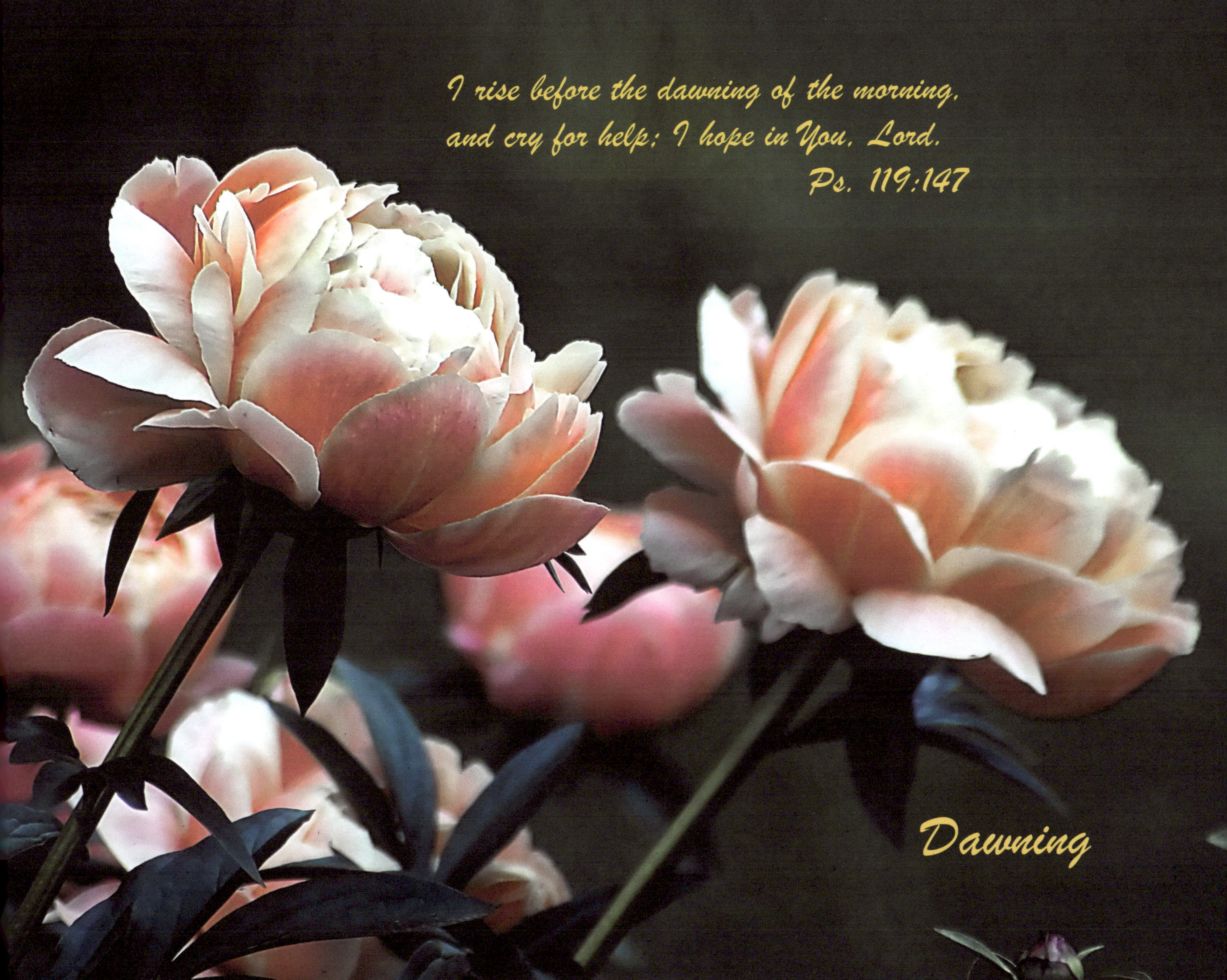
I rise before the dawning of the morning,
and cry for help; I hope in You, Lord.
Ps. 119:147
Dawning

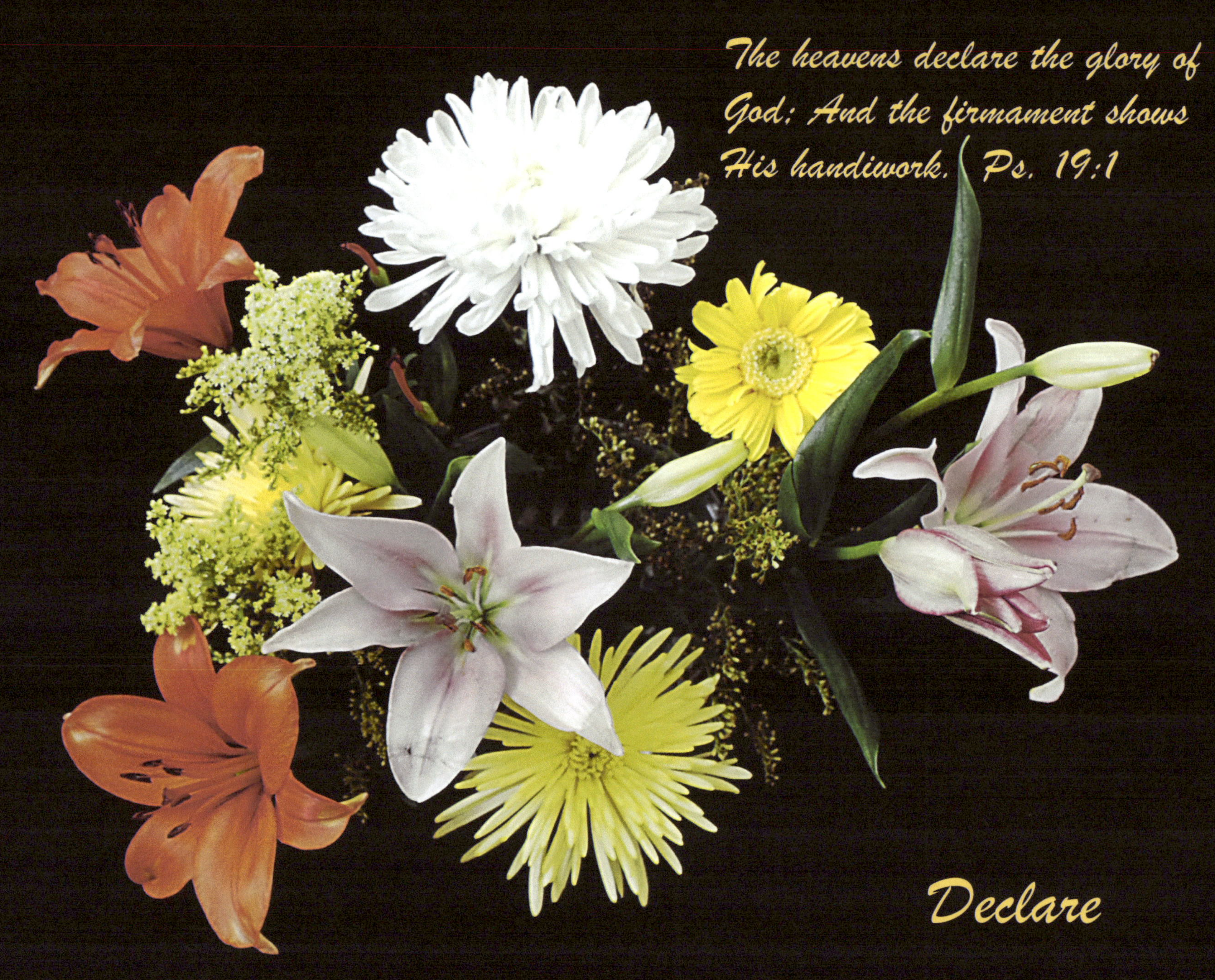
The heavens declare the glory of
God: And the firmament shows
His handiwork. Ps. 19:1
Declare

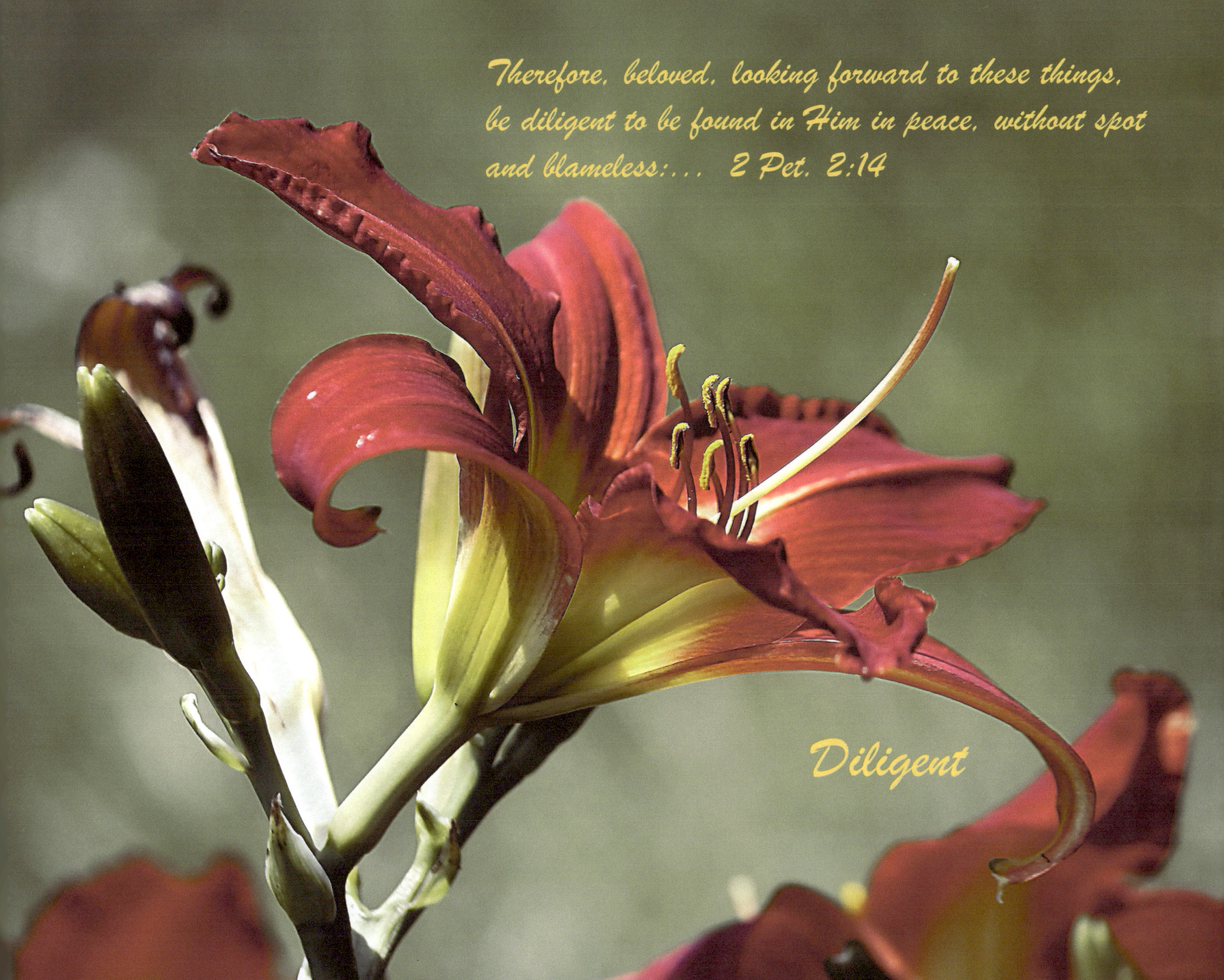
Therefore, beloved, looking forward to these things,
be diligent to be found in Him in peace, without spot
and blameless:... 2 Pet. 2:14
Diligent

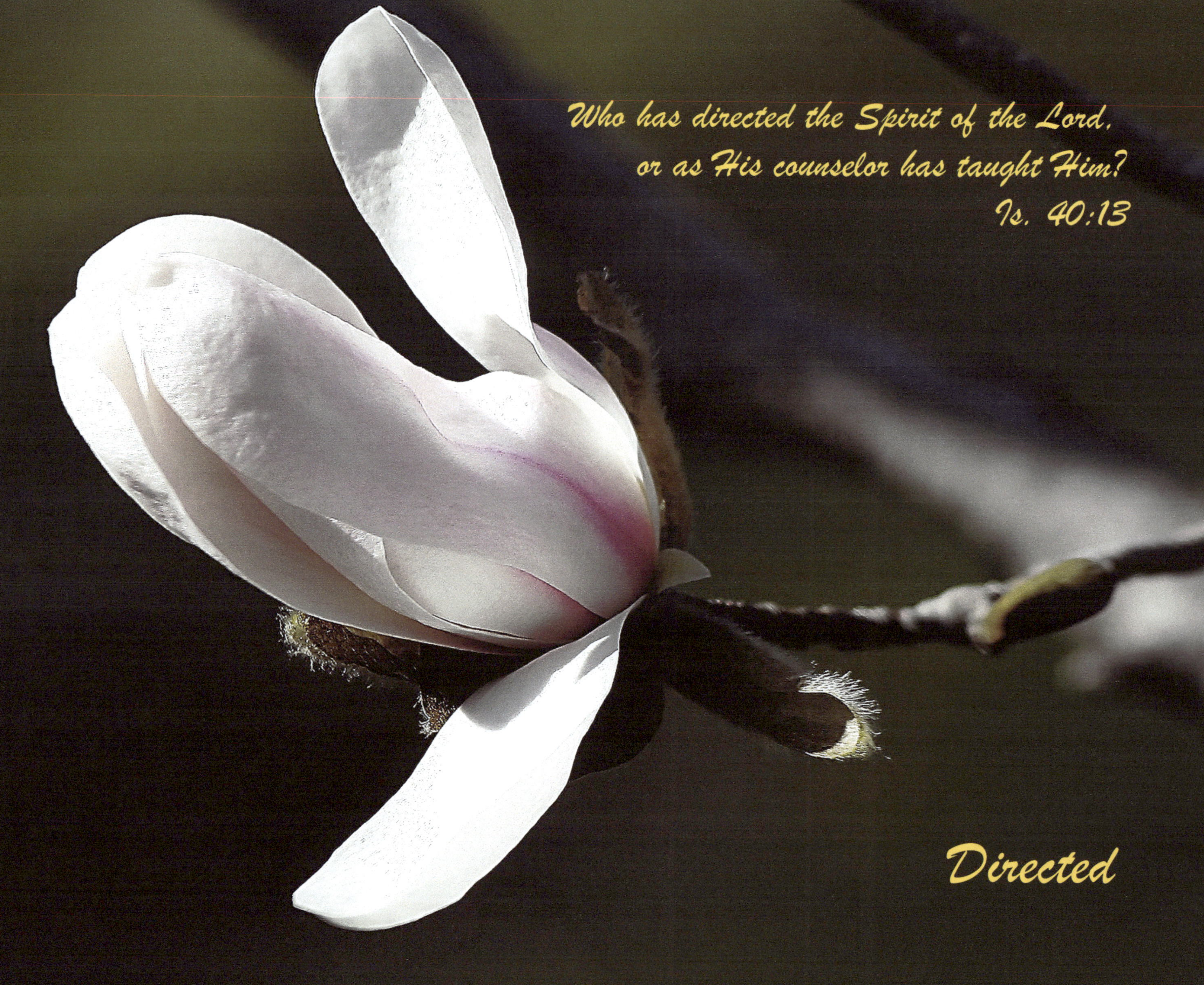
Who has directed the Spirit of the Lord,
or as His counselor has taught Him?
Is. 40:13
Directed

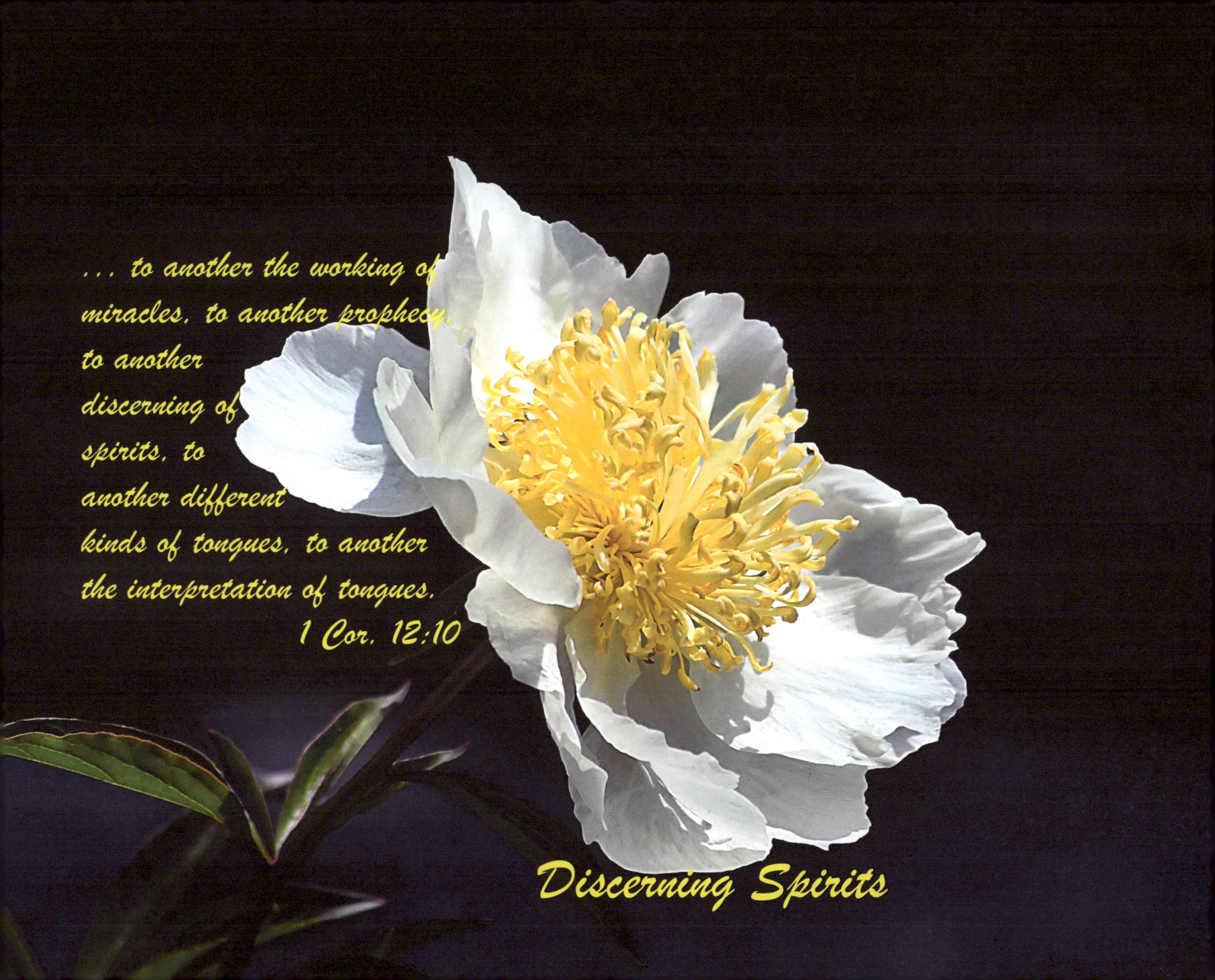

. . . to another the working of miracles, to another prophecy, to another discerning of spirits, to another different kinds of tongues, to another the interpretation of tongues.

1 Cor. 12:10

Discerning Spirits

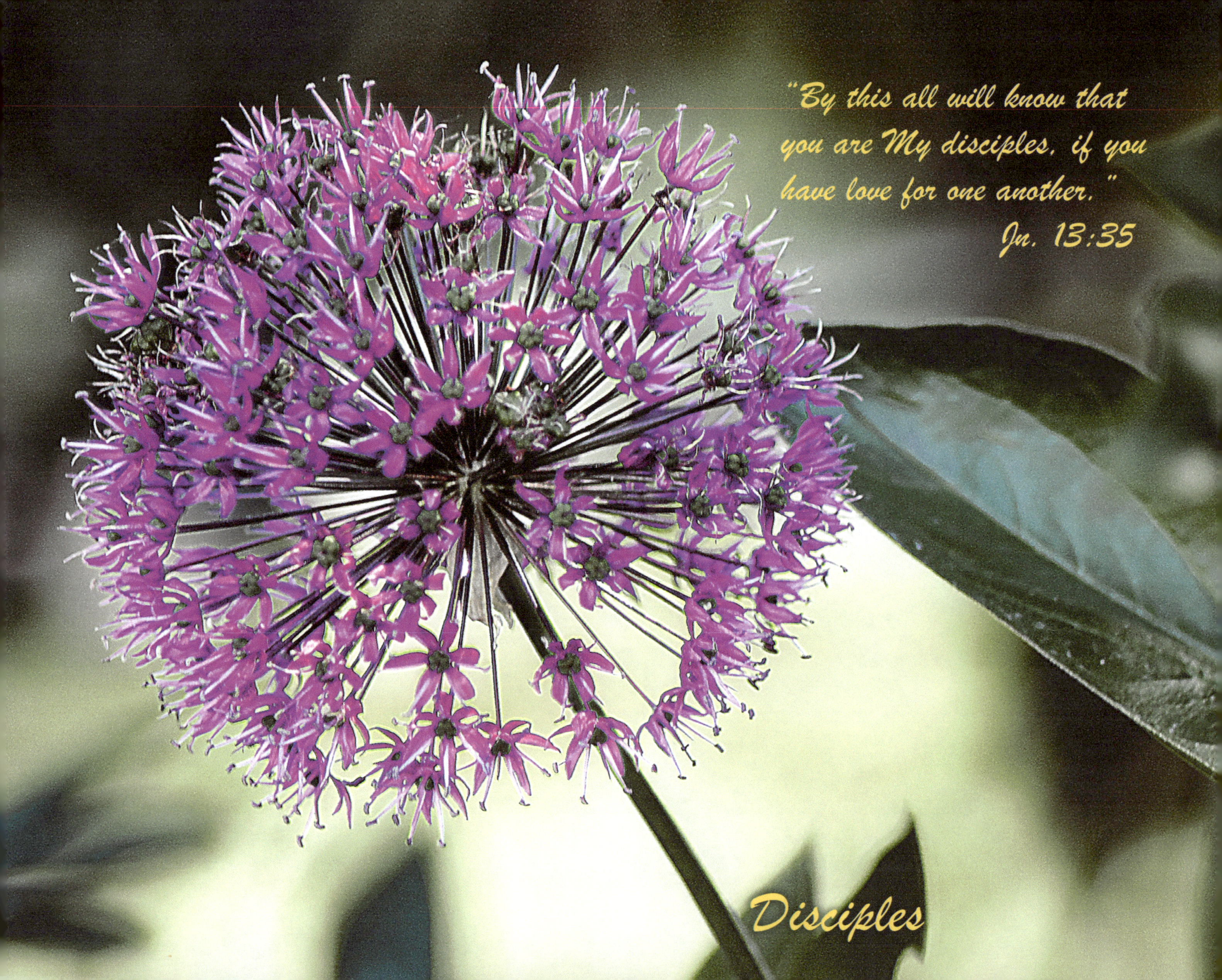
"By this all will know that
you are My disciples, if you
have love for one another."
Jn. 13:35
Disciples

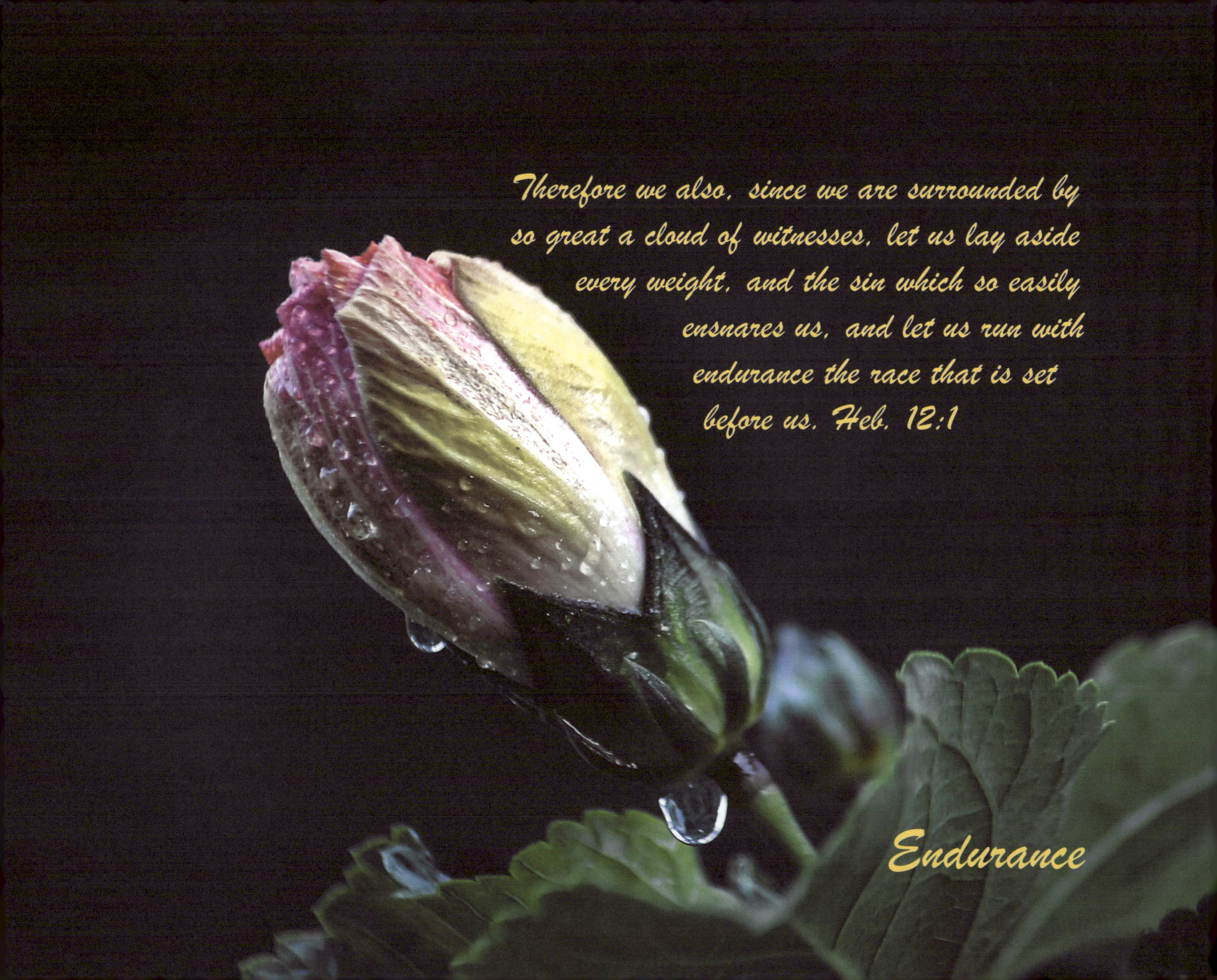

Therefore we also, since we are surrounded by so great a cloud of witnesses, let us lay aside every weight, and the sin which so easily ensnares us, and let us run with endurance the race that is set before us. Heb. 12:1

Endurance

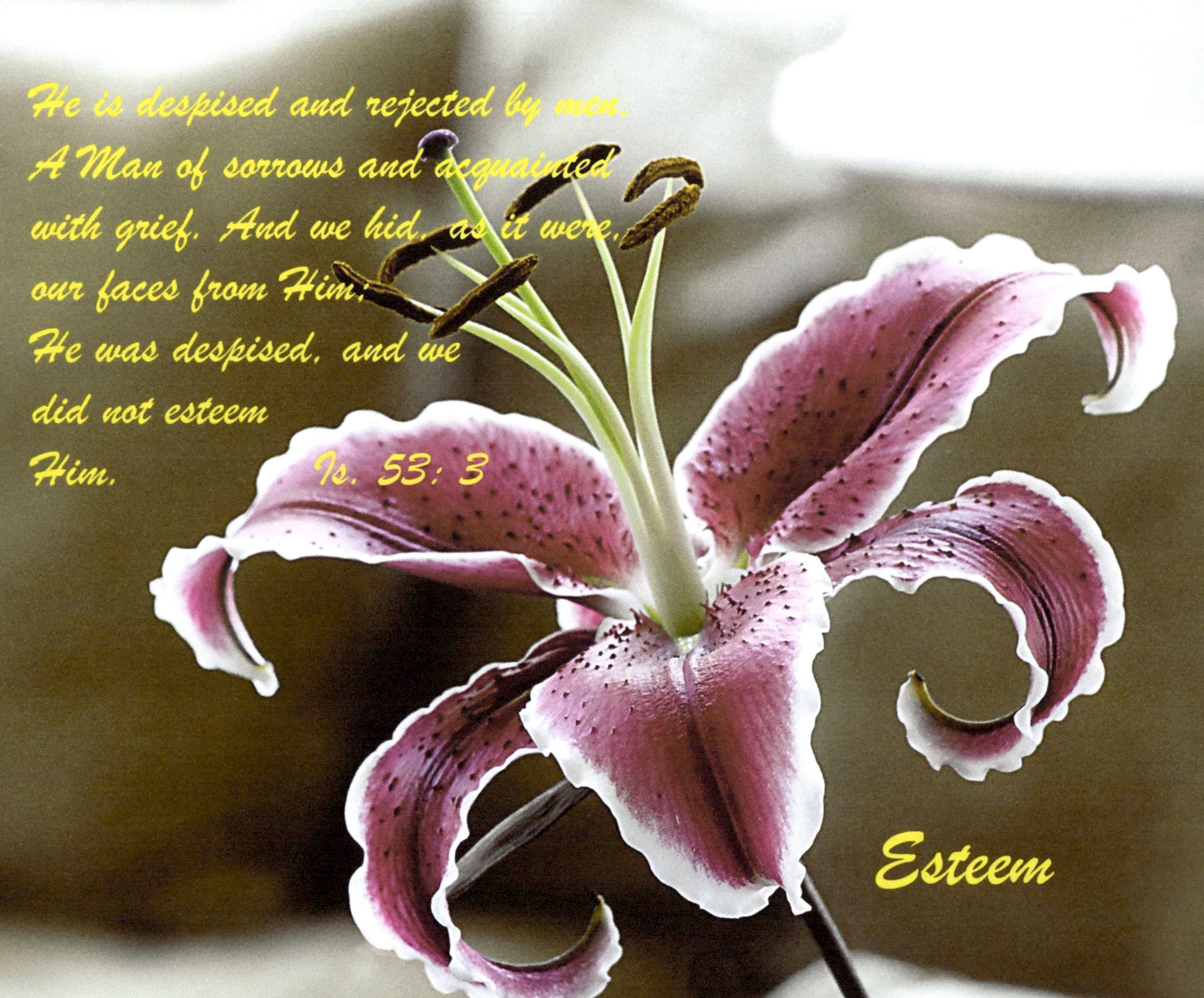
He is despised and rejected by men.
A Man of sorrows and acquainted
with grief. And we hid, as it were,
our faces from Him;
He was despised, and we
did not esteem
Him.
Is. 53: 3
Esteem

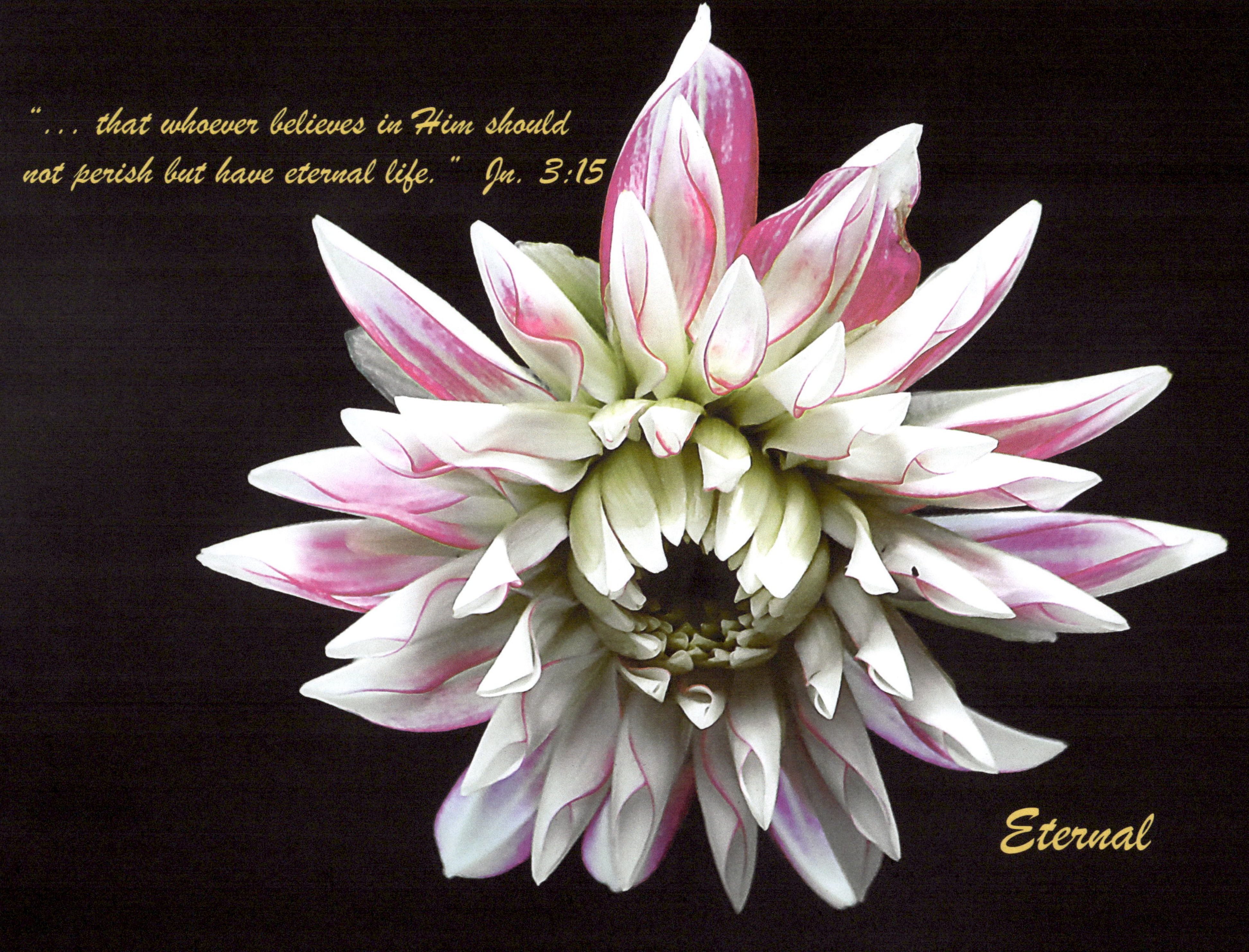
"... that whoever believes in Him should
not perish but have eternal life." Jn. 3:15
Eternal

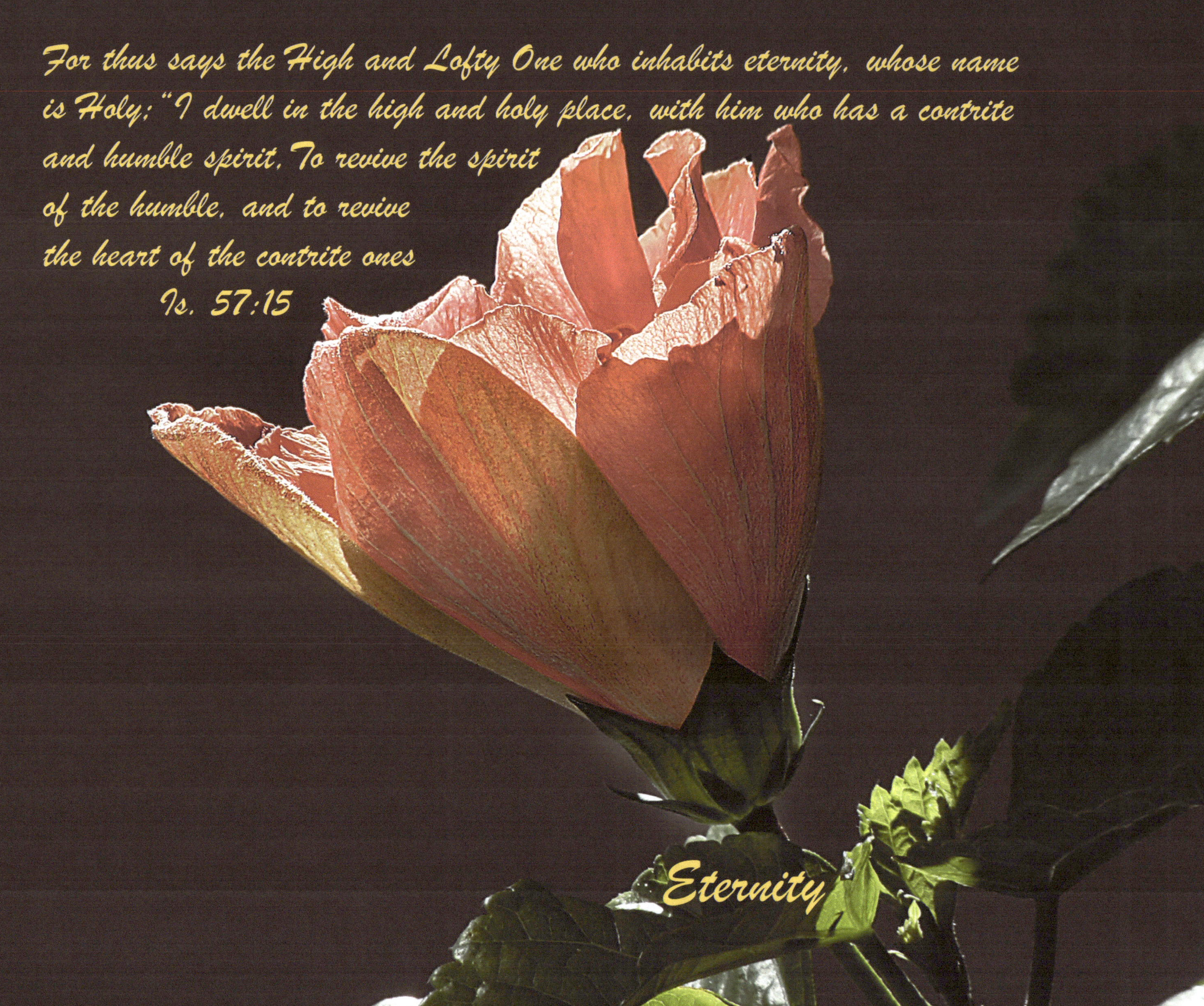
For thus says the High and Lofty One who inhabits eternity, whose name is Holy; "I dwell in the high and holy place, with him who has a contrite and humble spirit, To revive the spirit of the humble, and to revive the heart of the contrite ones
Is. 57:15
Eternity

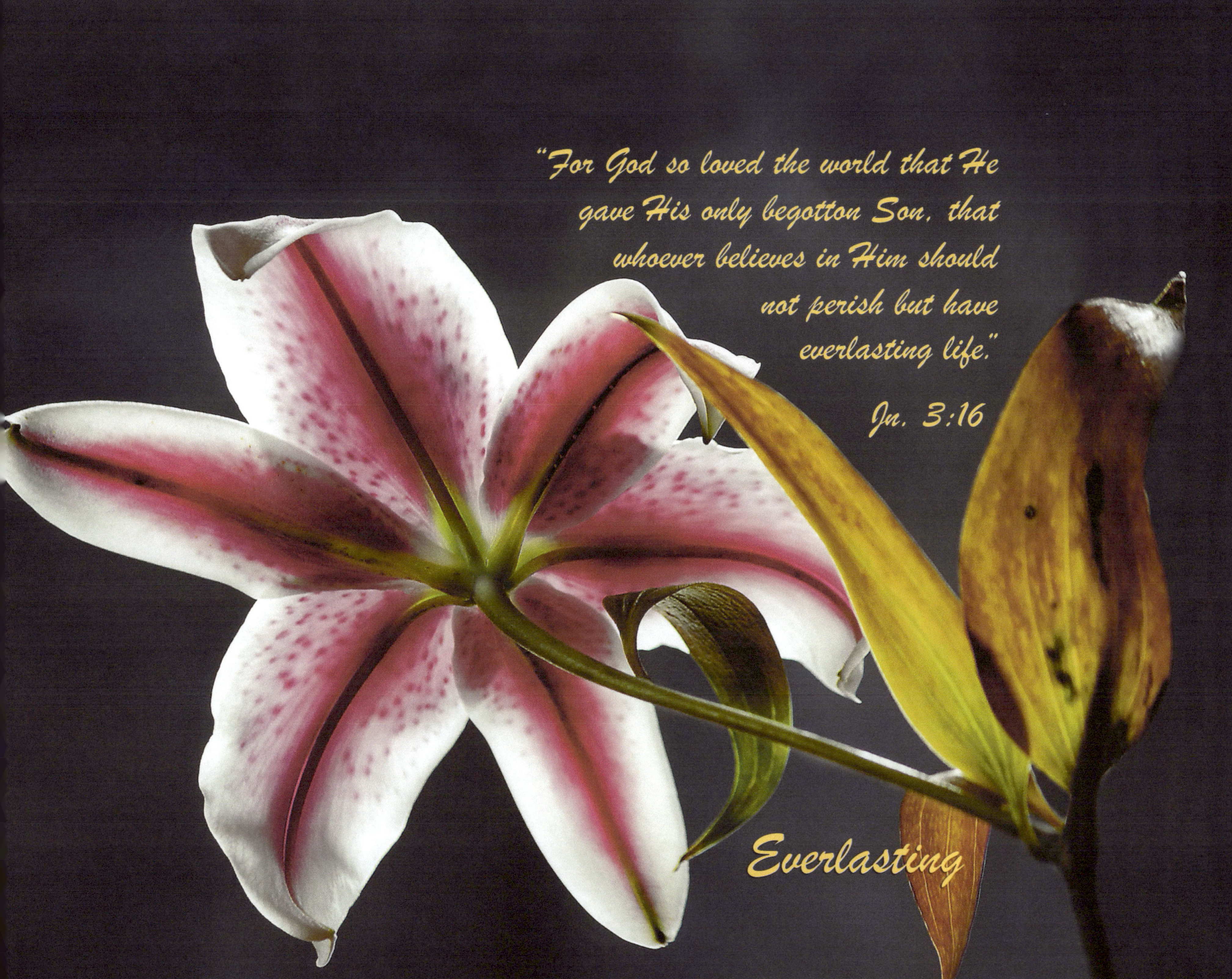
"For God so loved the world that He
gave His only begotton Son, that
whoever believes in Him should
not perish but have
everlasting life."
Jn. 3:16
Everlasting

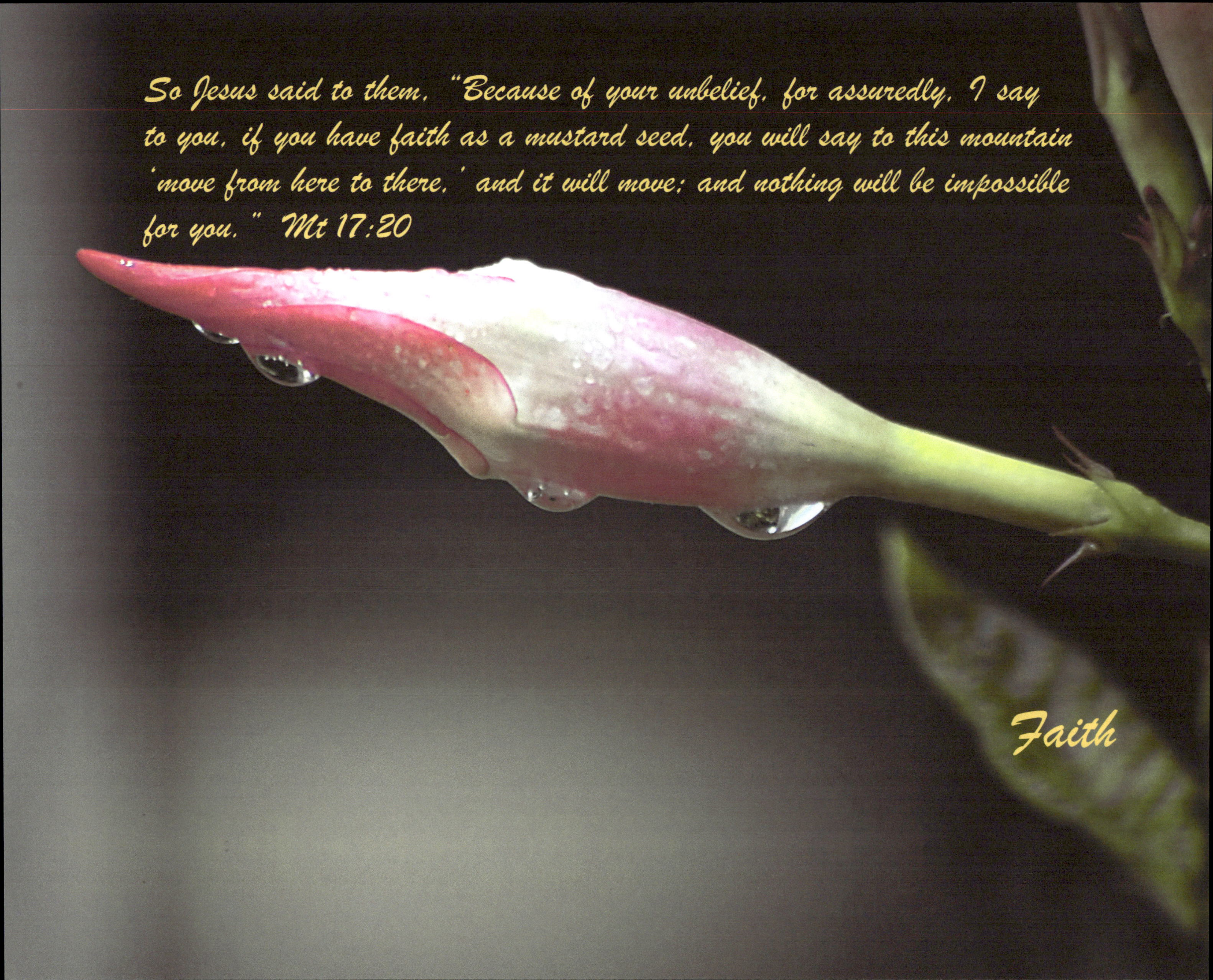

So Jesus said to them, "Because of your unbelief, for assuredly, I say to you, if you have faith as a mustard seed, you will say to this mountain 'move from here to there,' and it will move; and nothing will be impossible for you." Mt 17:20

Faith

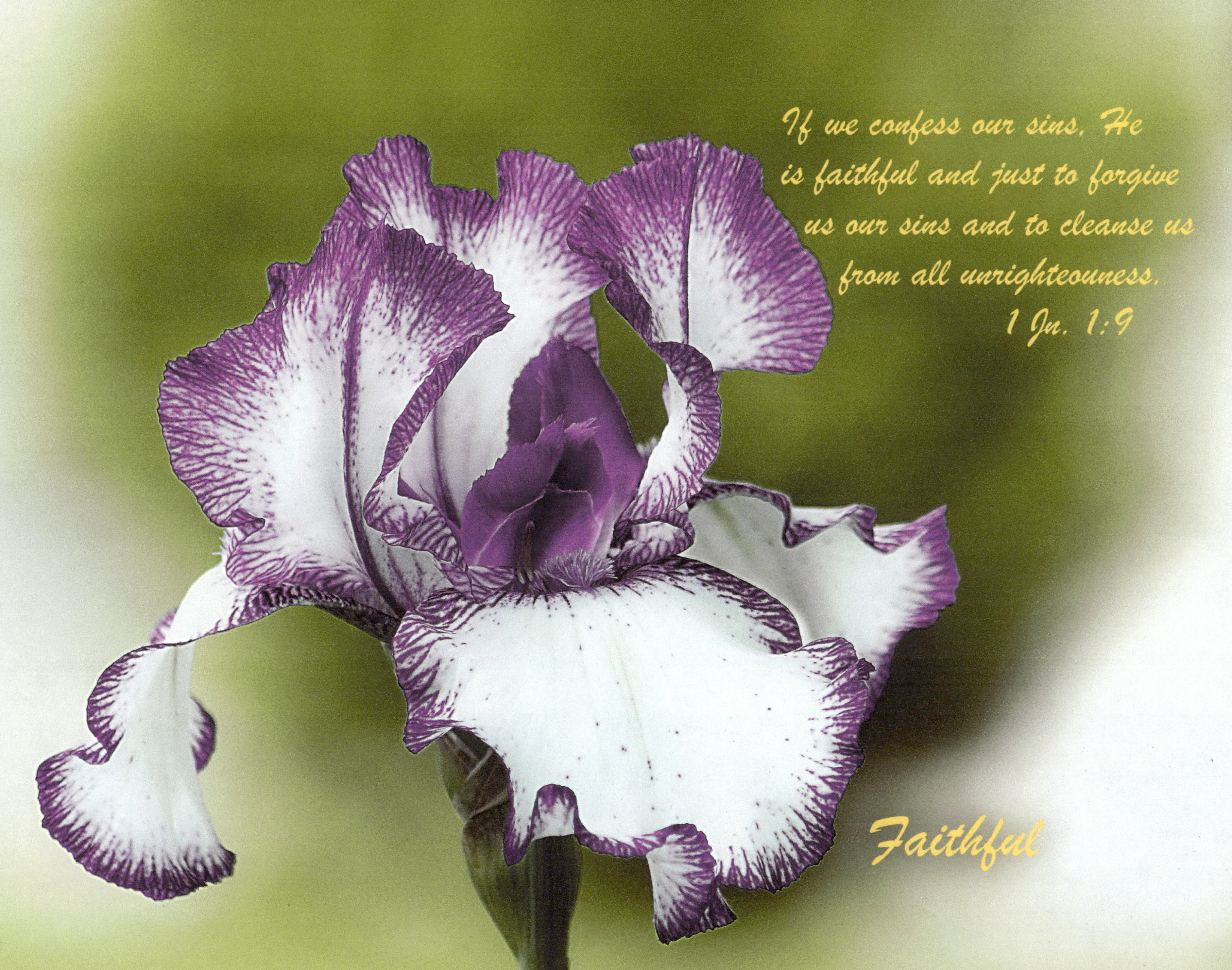
If we confess our sins, He
is faithful and just to forgive
us our sins and to cleanse us
from all unrighteouness.
1 Jn. 1:9
Faithful

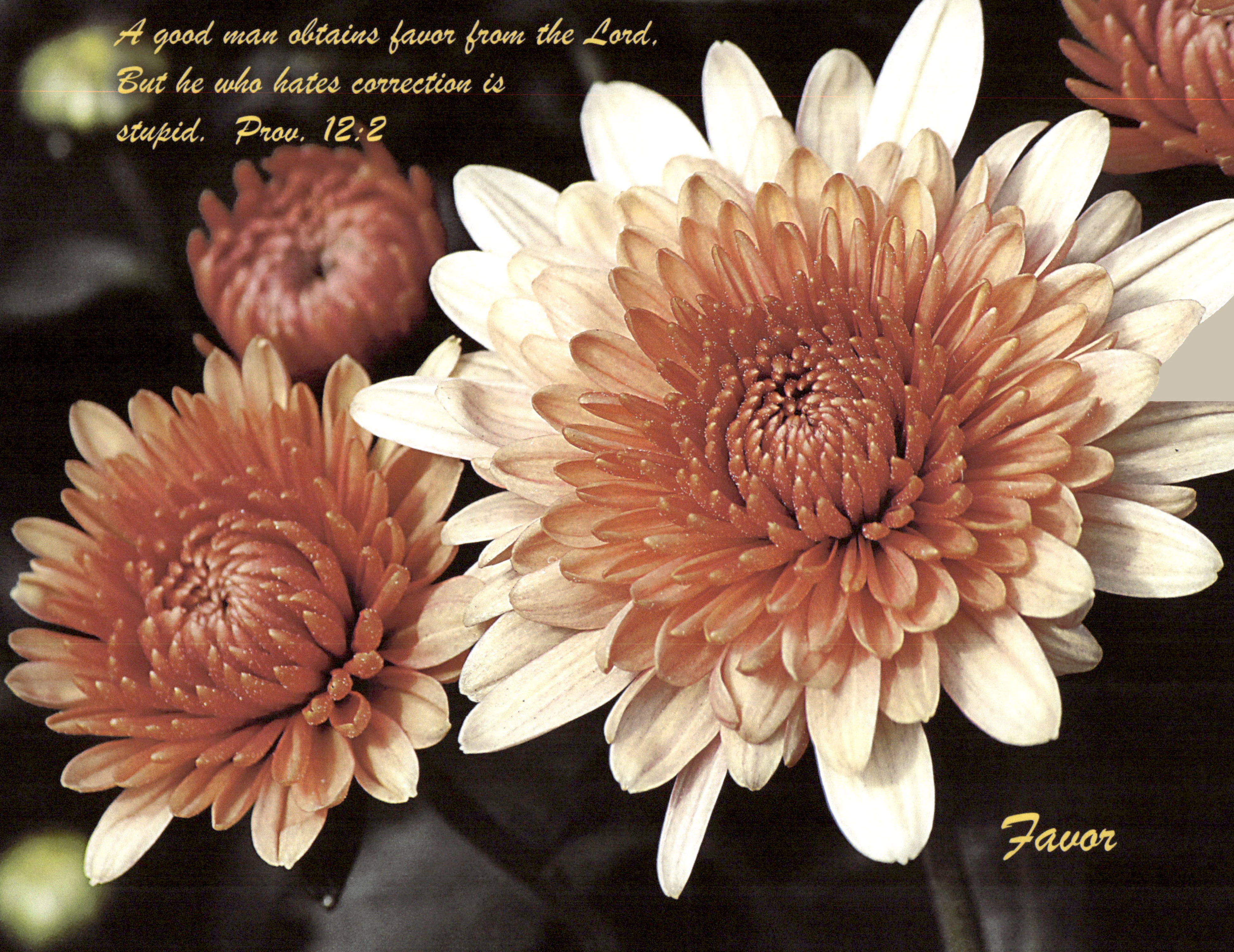
A good man obtains favor from the Lord,
But he who hates correction is
stupid. Prov. 12:2
Favor

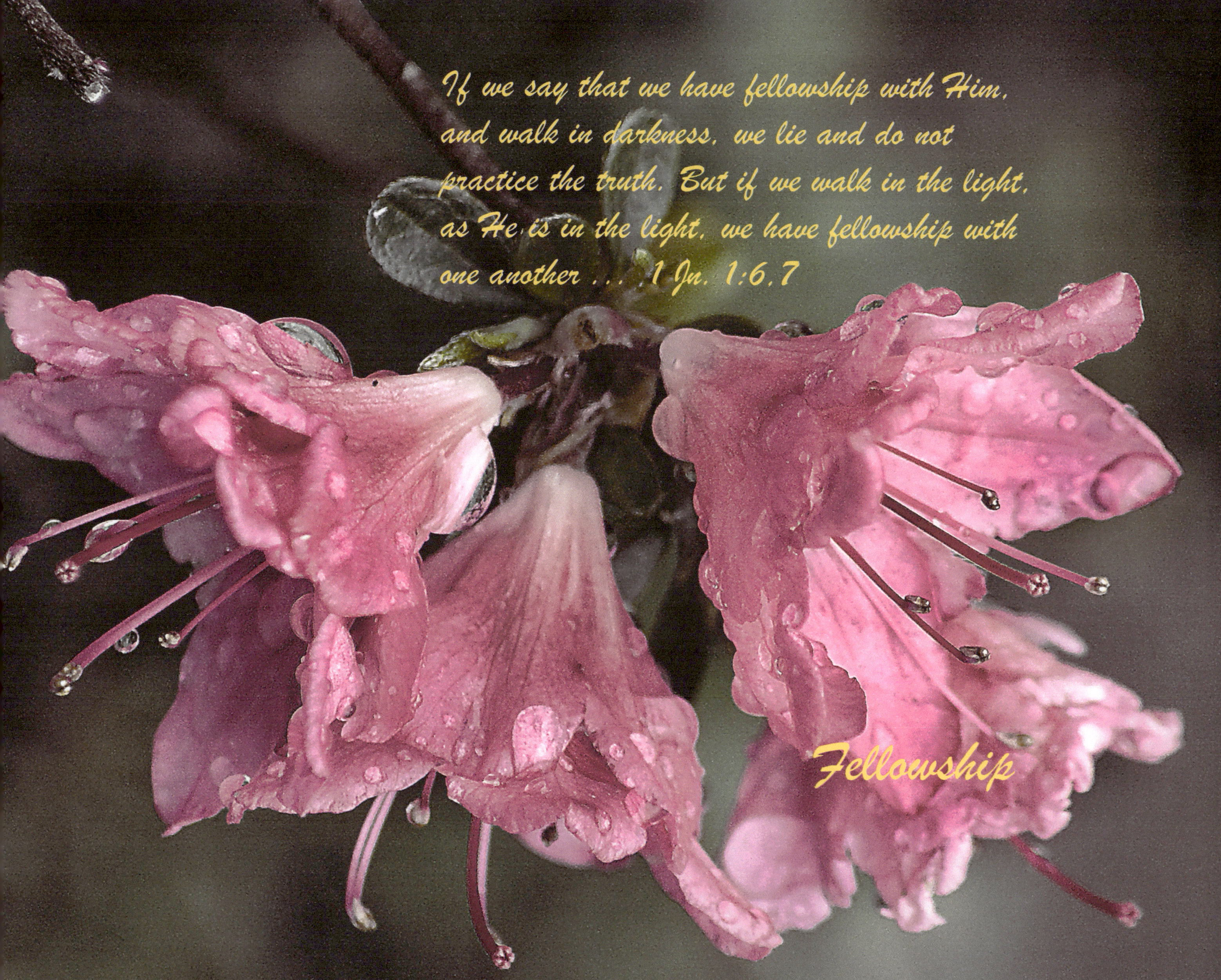
If we say that we have fellowship with Him,
and walk in darkness, we lie and do not
practice the truth. But if we walk in the light,
as He is in the light, we have fellowship with
one another . . . 1 Jn. 1:6,7
Fellowship

"If My people who are called by My name will humble themselves, and pray and seek My face, and turn from their wicked ways, then I will hear from heaven, and will forgive their sin and heal their land." 2 Chr. 7:14

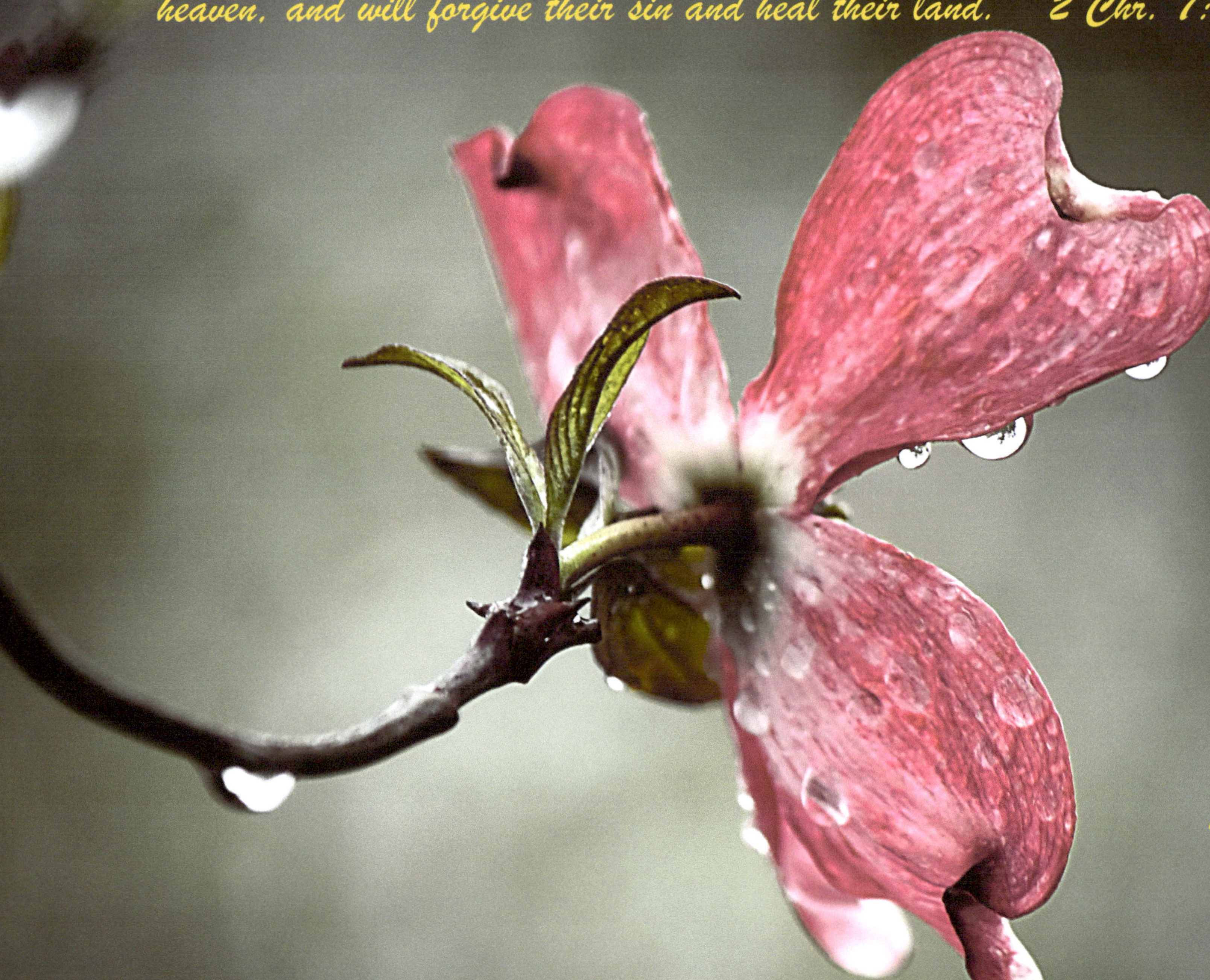

Forgive

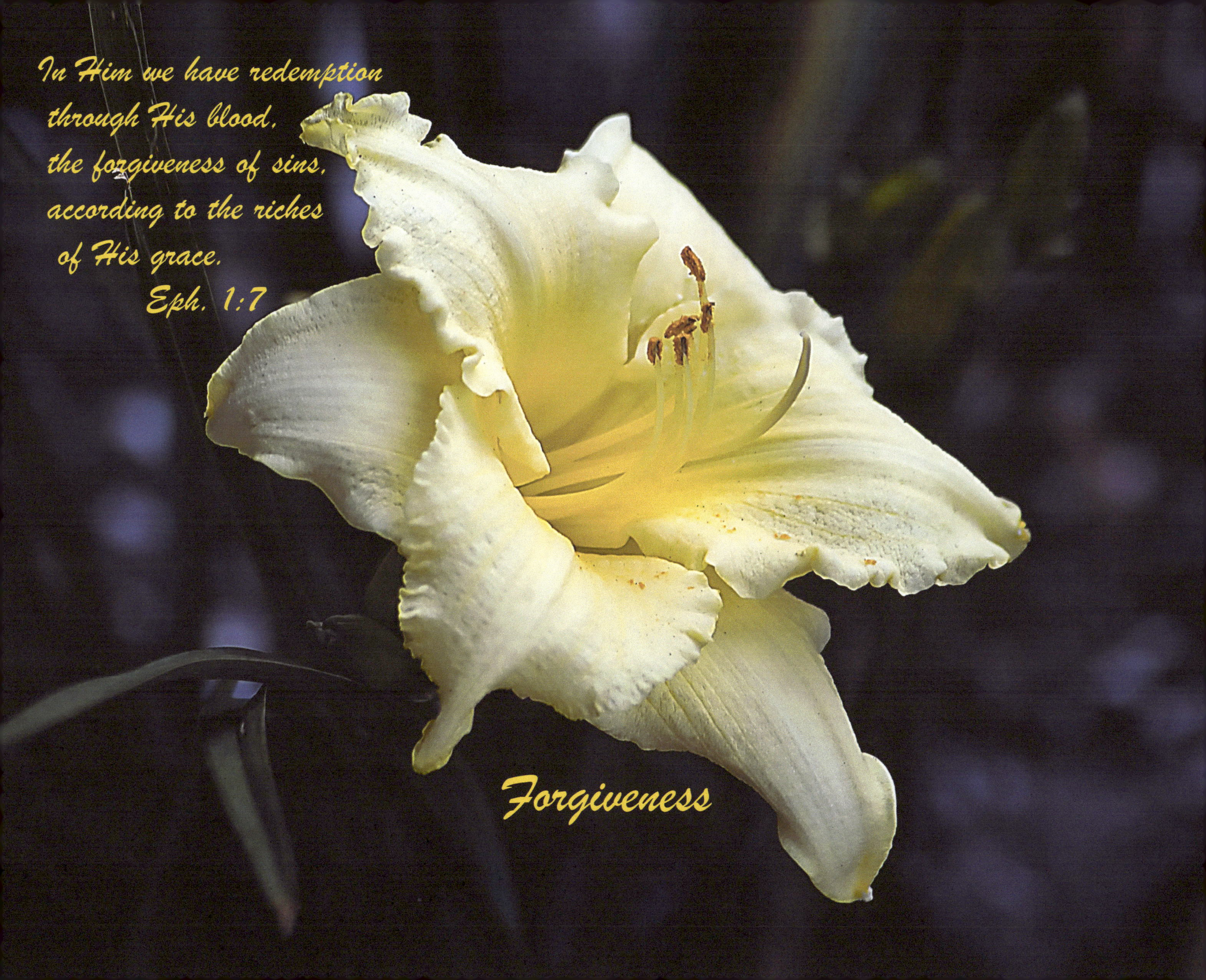

In Him we have redemption
through His blood,
the forgiveness of sins,
according to the riches
of His grace.
Eph. 1:7

Forgiveness

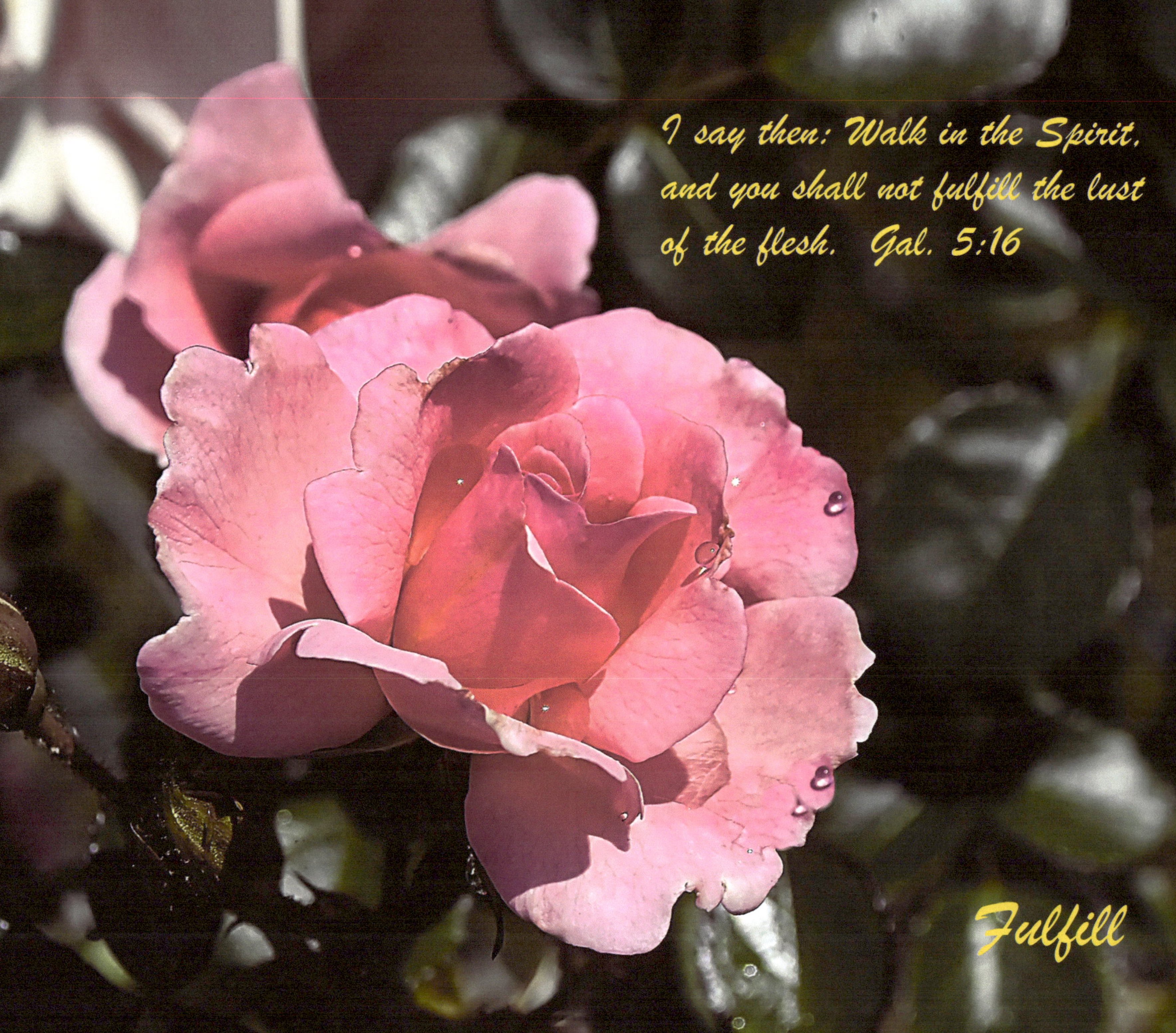
I say then: Walk in the Spirit, and you shall not fulfill the lust of the flesh. Gal. 5:16
Fulfill

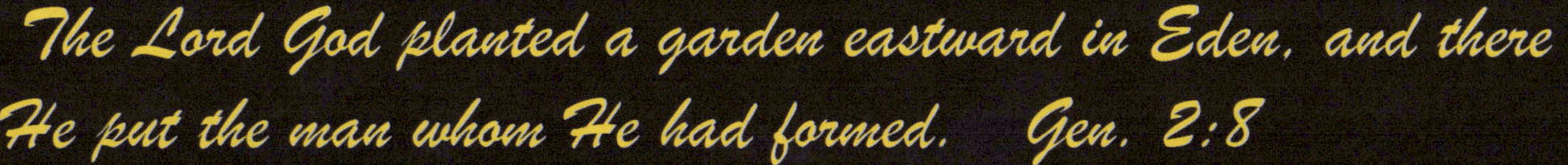

The Lord God planted a garden eastward in Eden, and there He put the man whom He had formed. Gen. 2:8

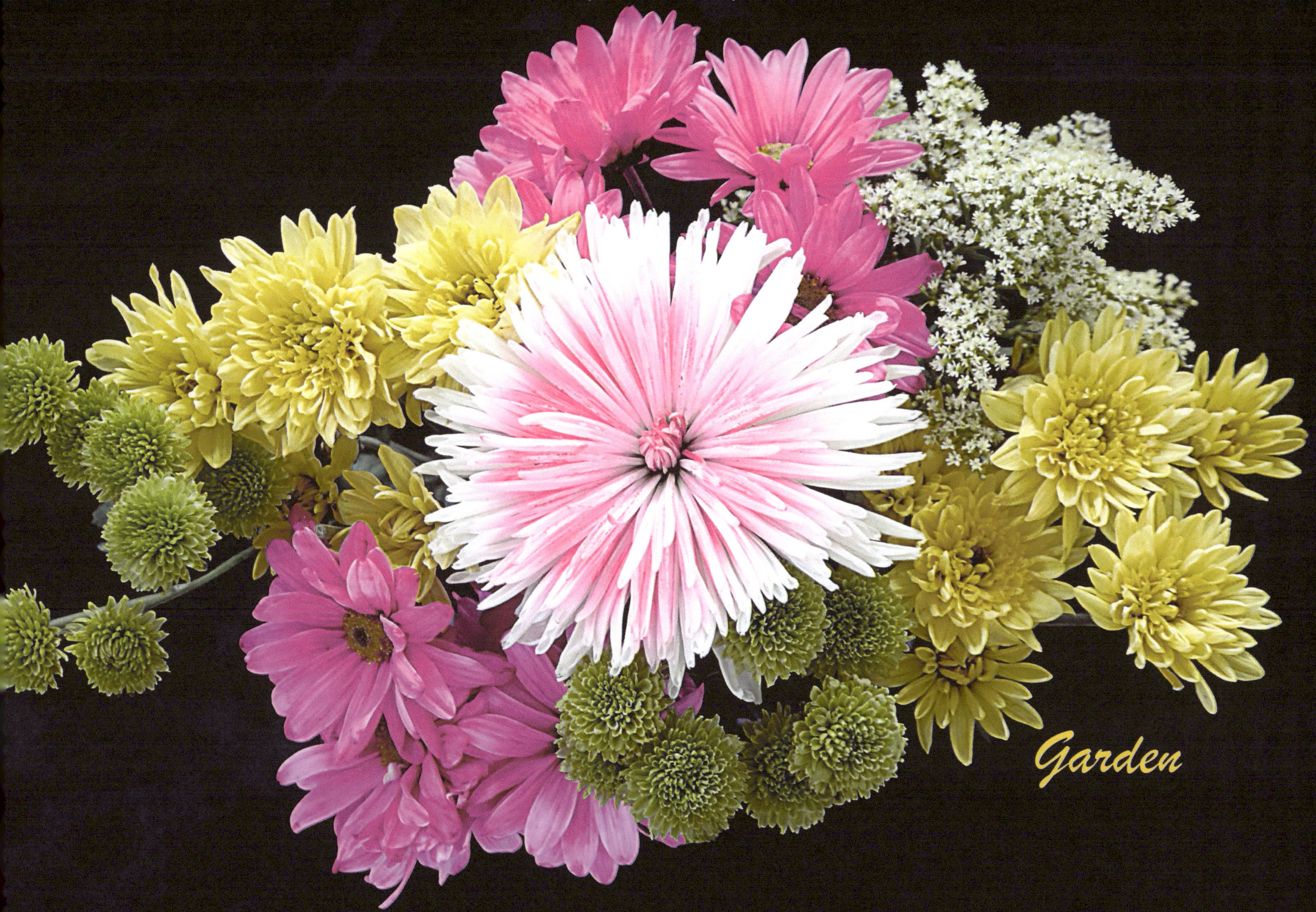

Garden

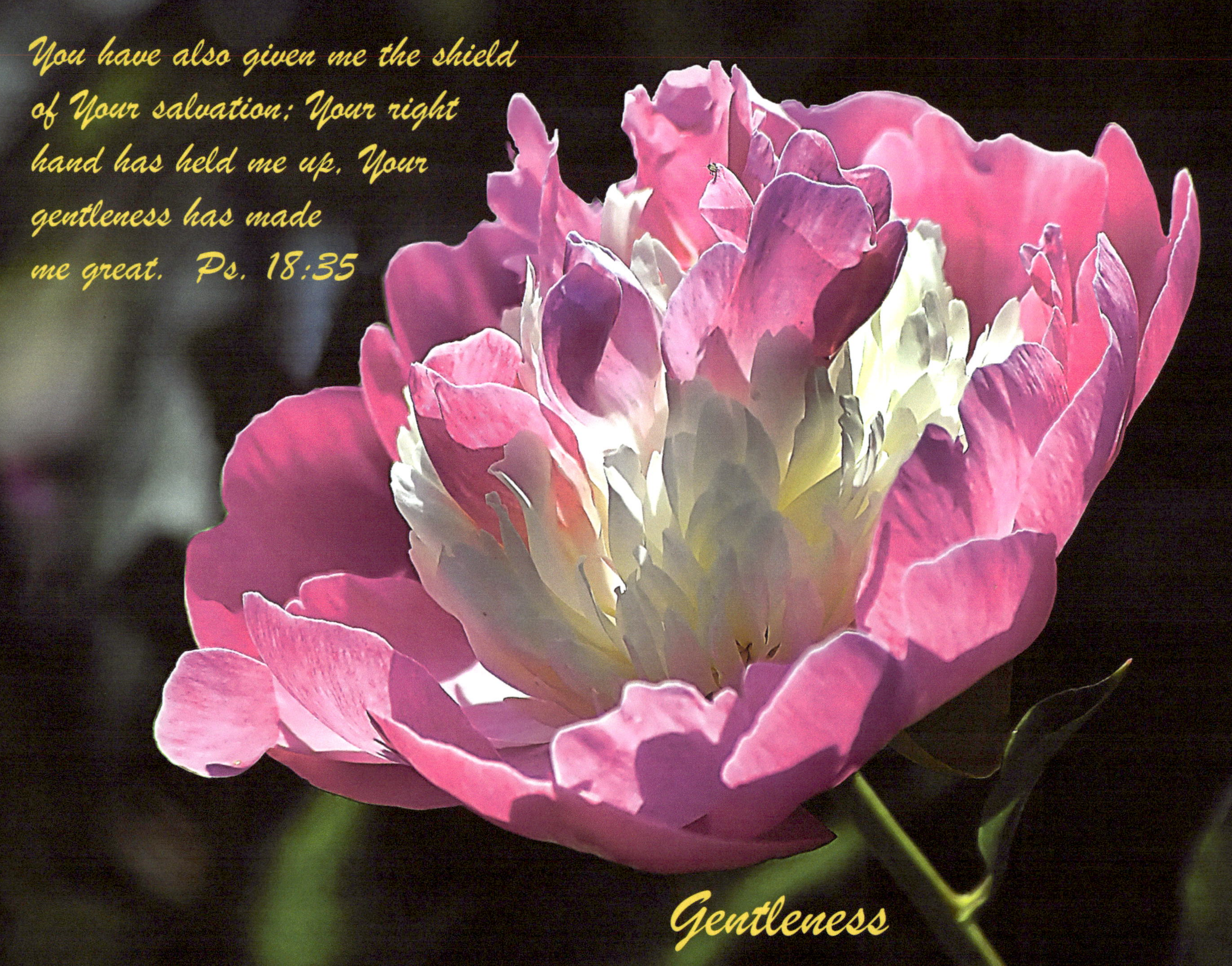
You have also given me the shield
of Your salvation; Your right
hand has held me up, Your
gentleness has made
me great. Ps. 18:35
Gentleness

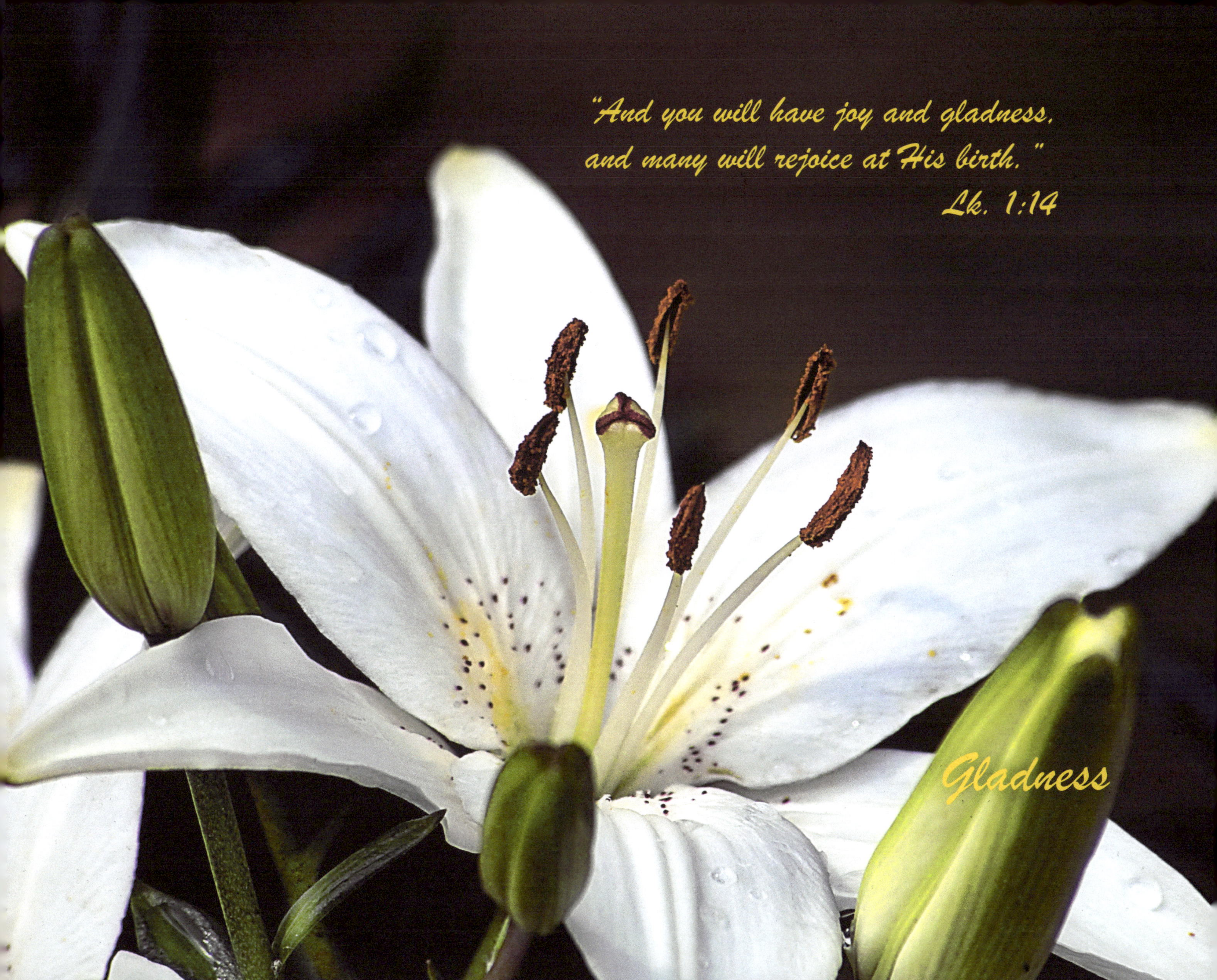
"And you will have joy and gladness,
and many will rejoice at His birth."
Lk. 1:14
Gladness

Surely goodness and mercy shall follow me All the days of my life;
And I will dwell in the house of the Lord Forever. Ps. 23:6

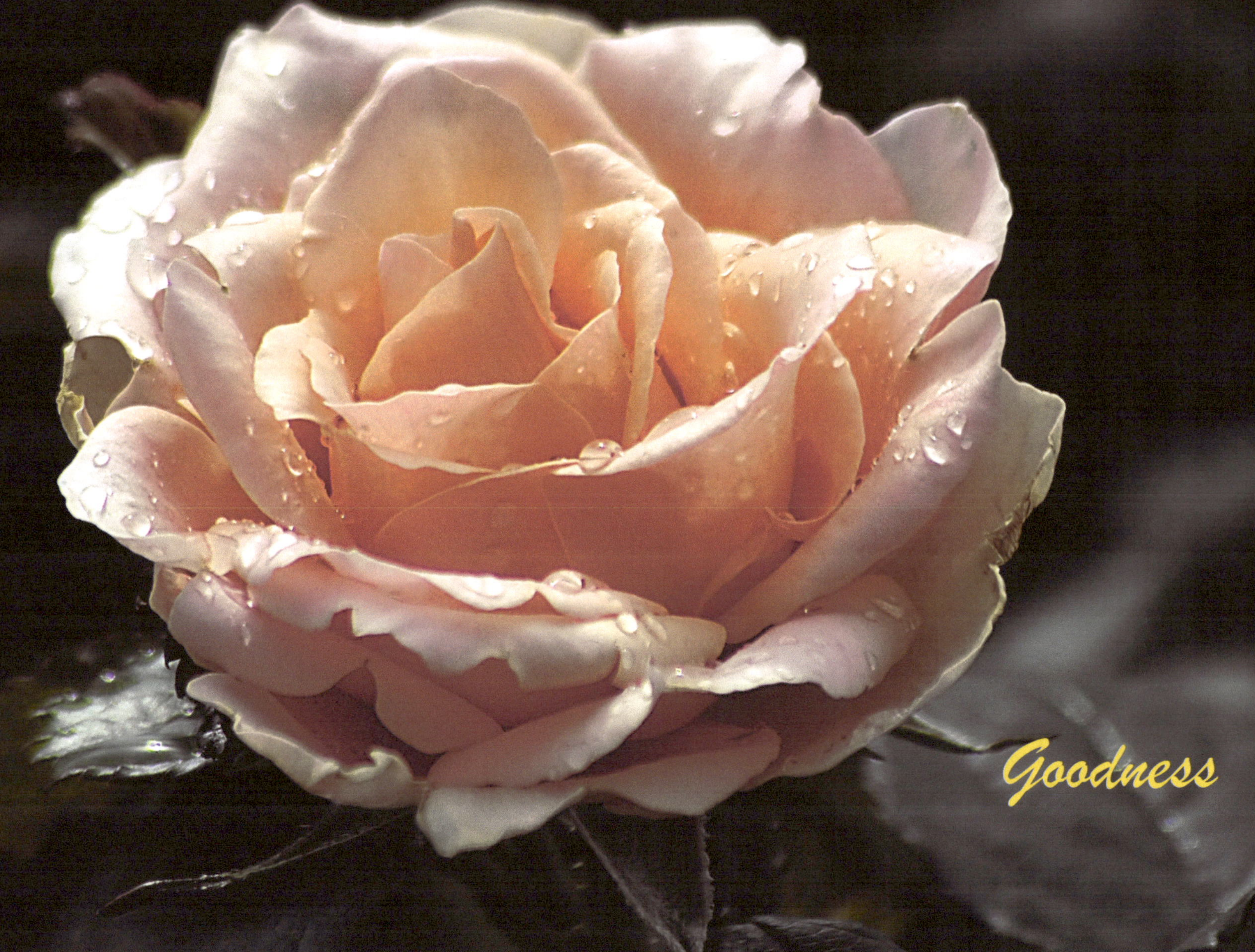

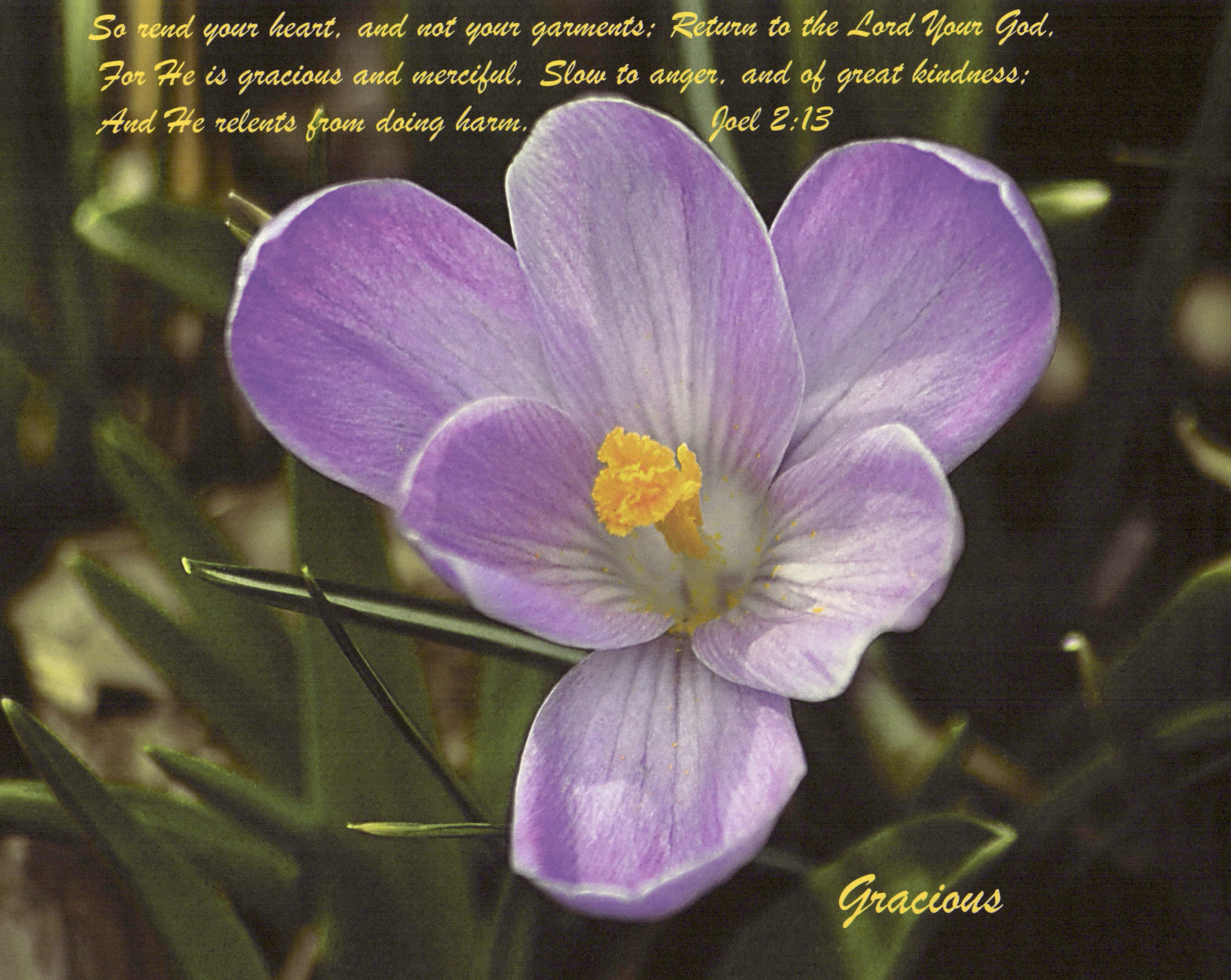
So rend your heart, and not your garments; Return to the Lord Your God,
For He is gracious and merciful, Slow to anger, and of great kindness;
And He relents from doing harm.
Joel 2:13
Gracious

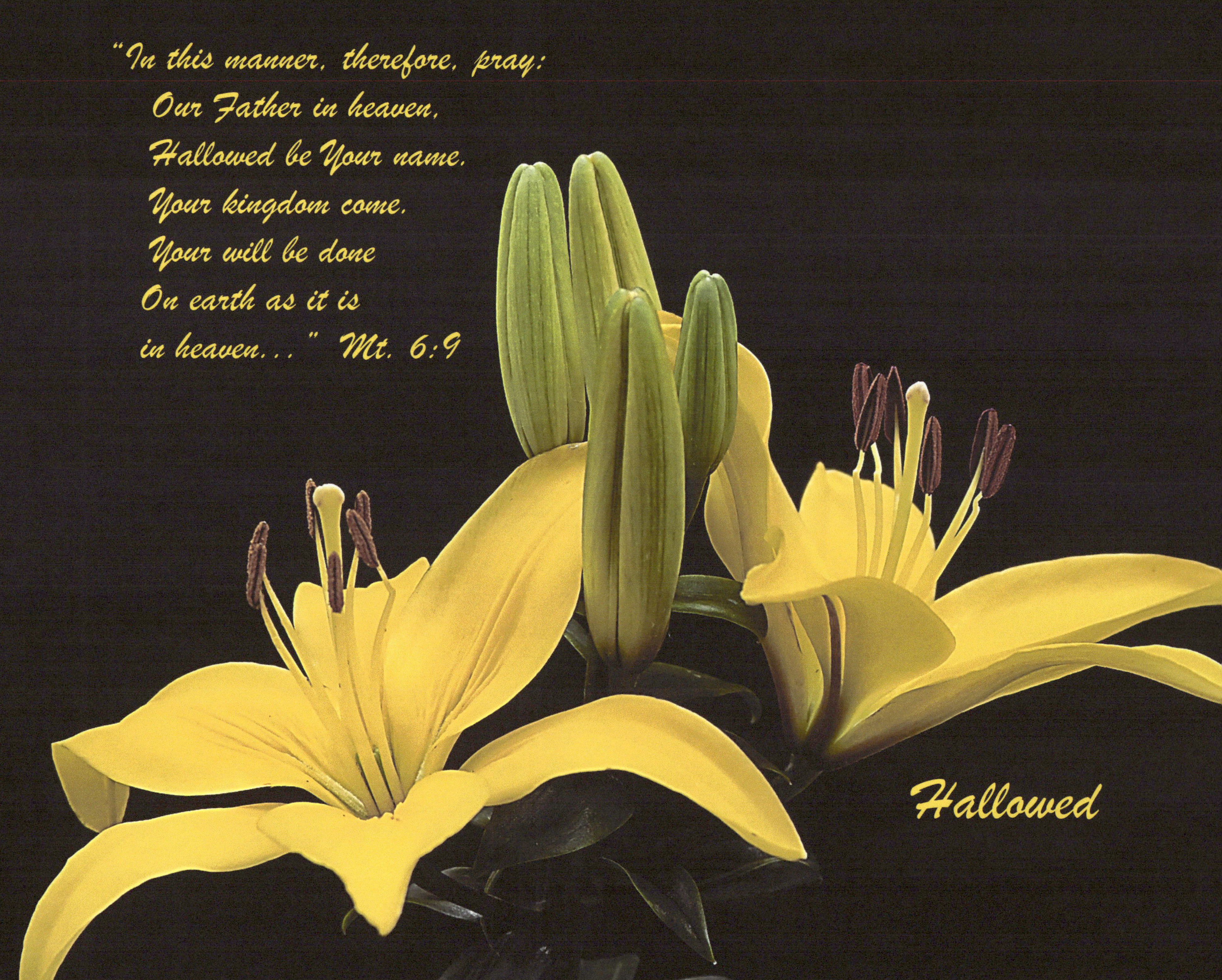
"In this manner, therefore, pray:
Our Father in heaven,
Hallowed be Your name,
Your kingdom come,
Your will be done
On earth as it is
in heaven..." Mt. 6:9
Hallowed

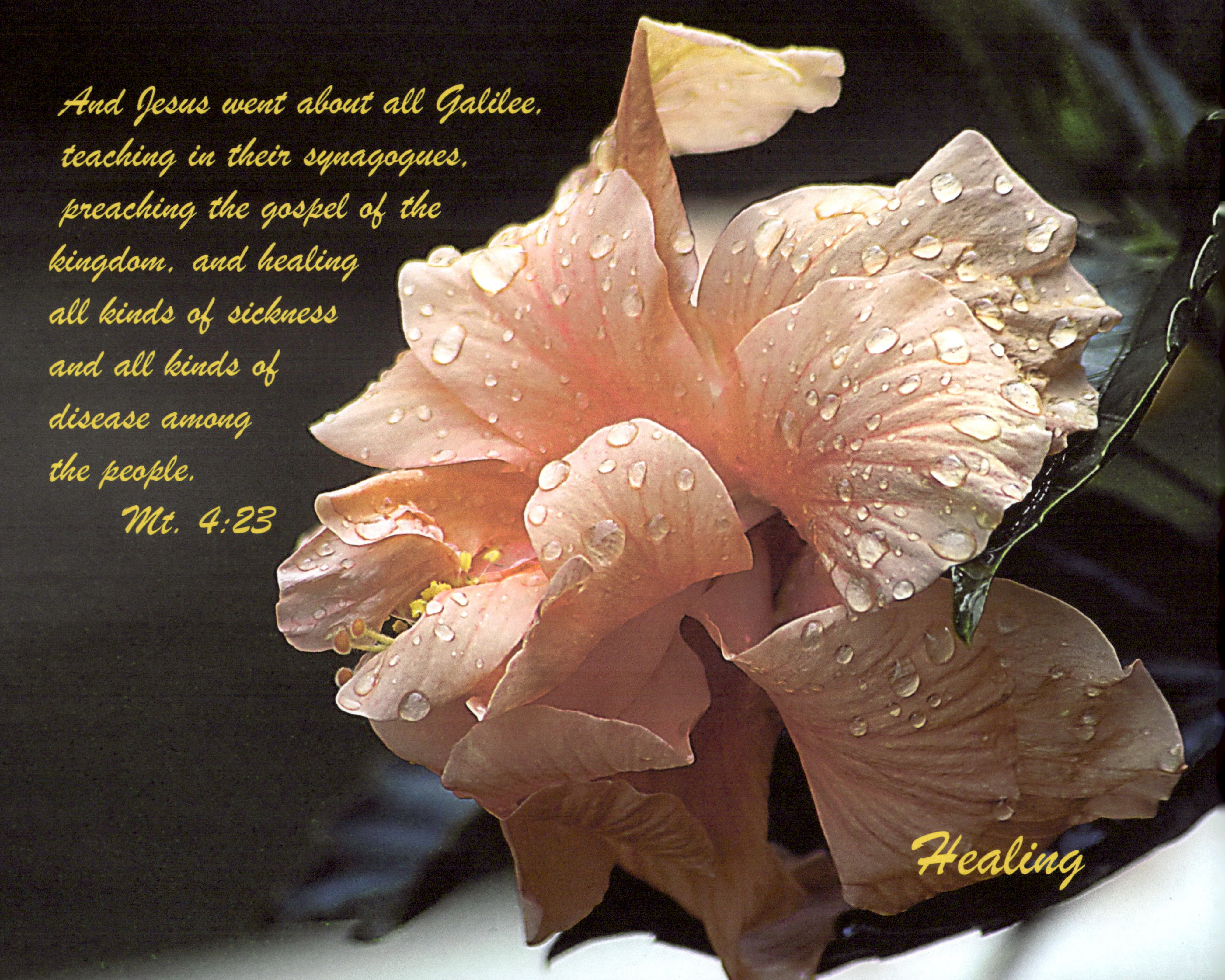
And Jesus went about all Galilee,
teaching in their synagogues,
preaching the gospel of the
kingdom, and healing
all kinds of sickness
and all kinds of
disease among
the people.
Mt. 4:23
Healing

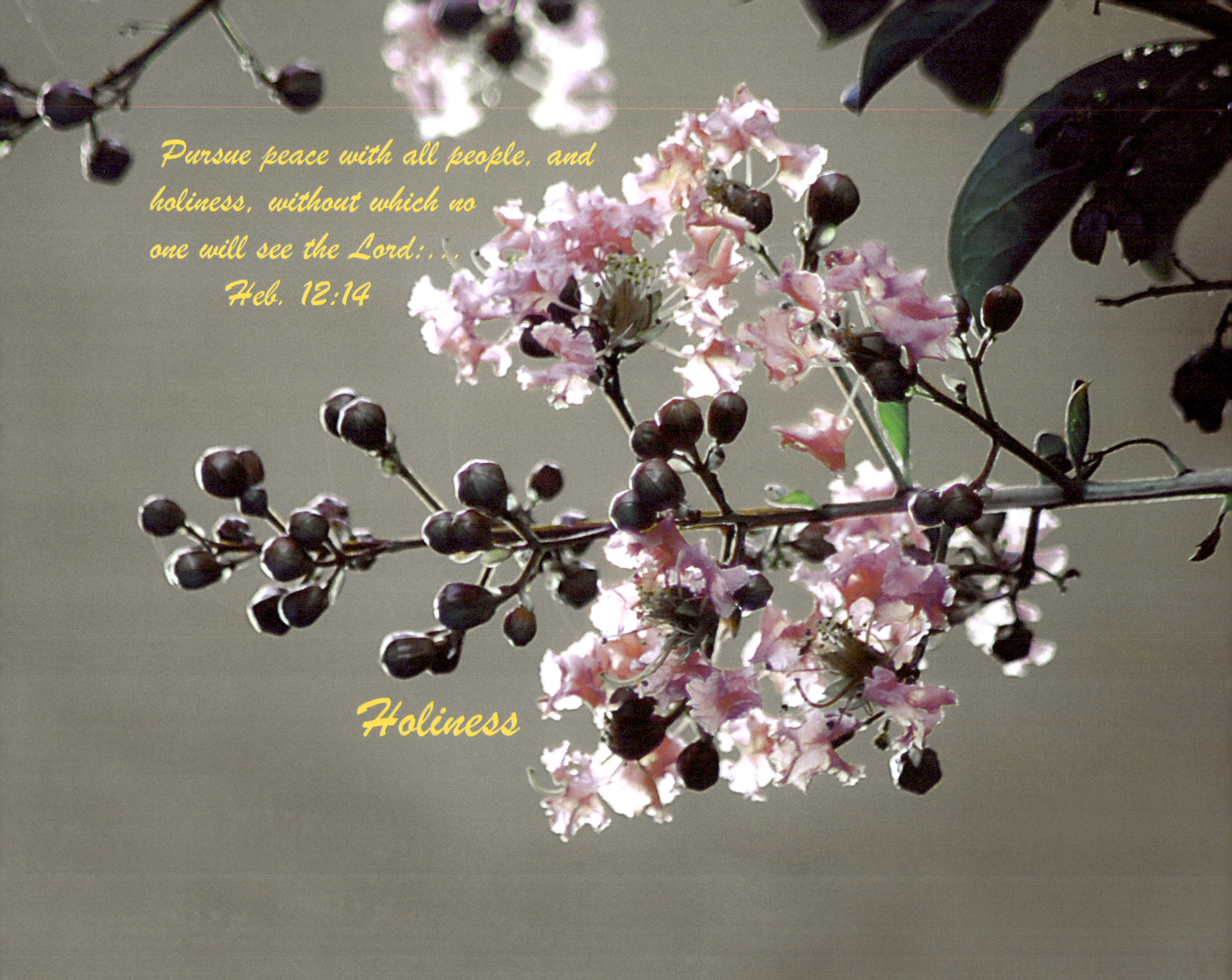
Pursue peace with all people, and
holiness, without which no
one will see the Lord:...
Heb. 12:14
Holiness

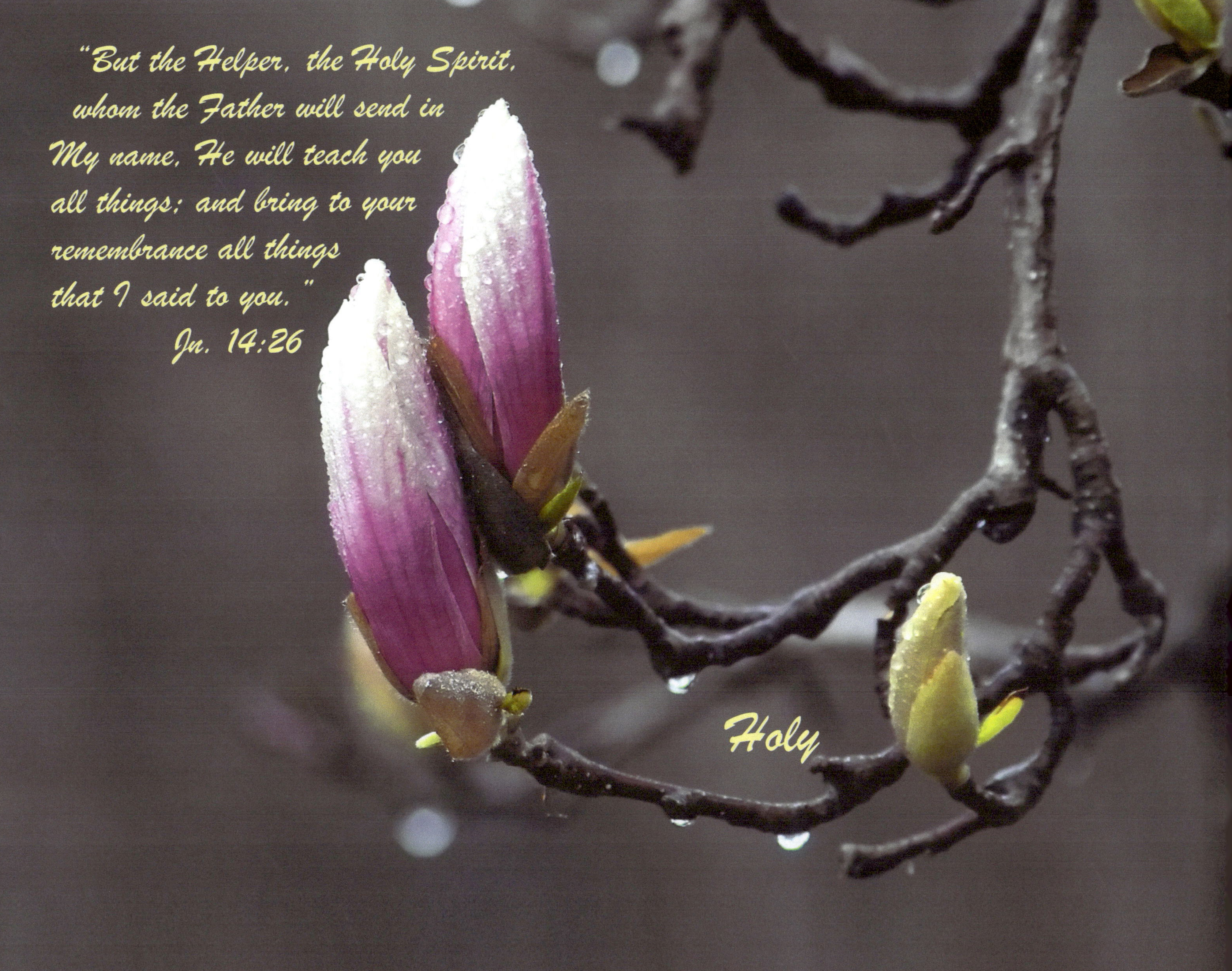
"But the Helper, the Holy Spirit,
whom the Father will send in
My name, He will teach you
all things; and bring to your
remembrance all things
that I said to you."
Jn. 14:26
Holy

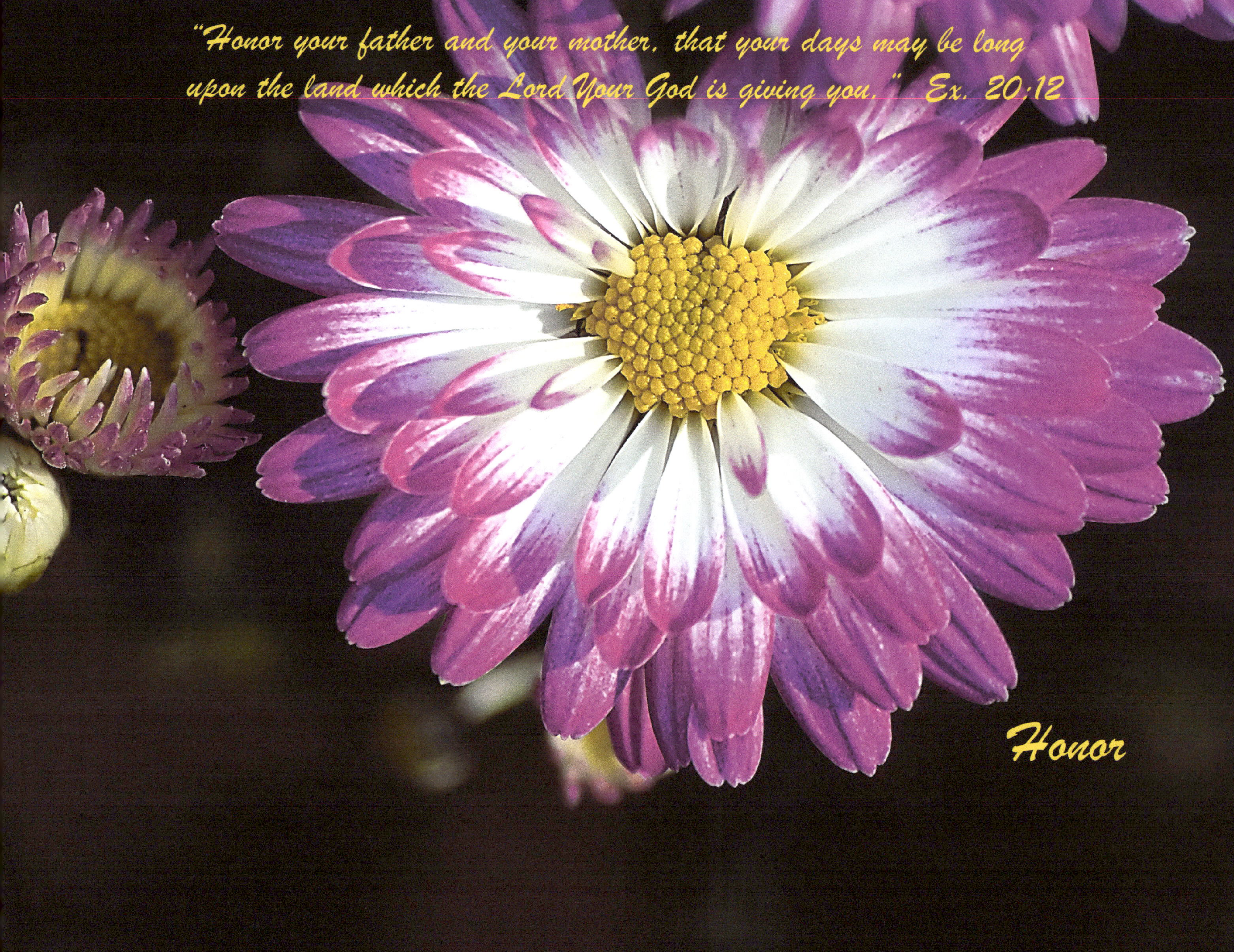
"Honor your father and your mother, that your days may be long
upon the land which the Lord Your God is giving you." Ex. 20:12
Honor

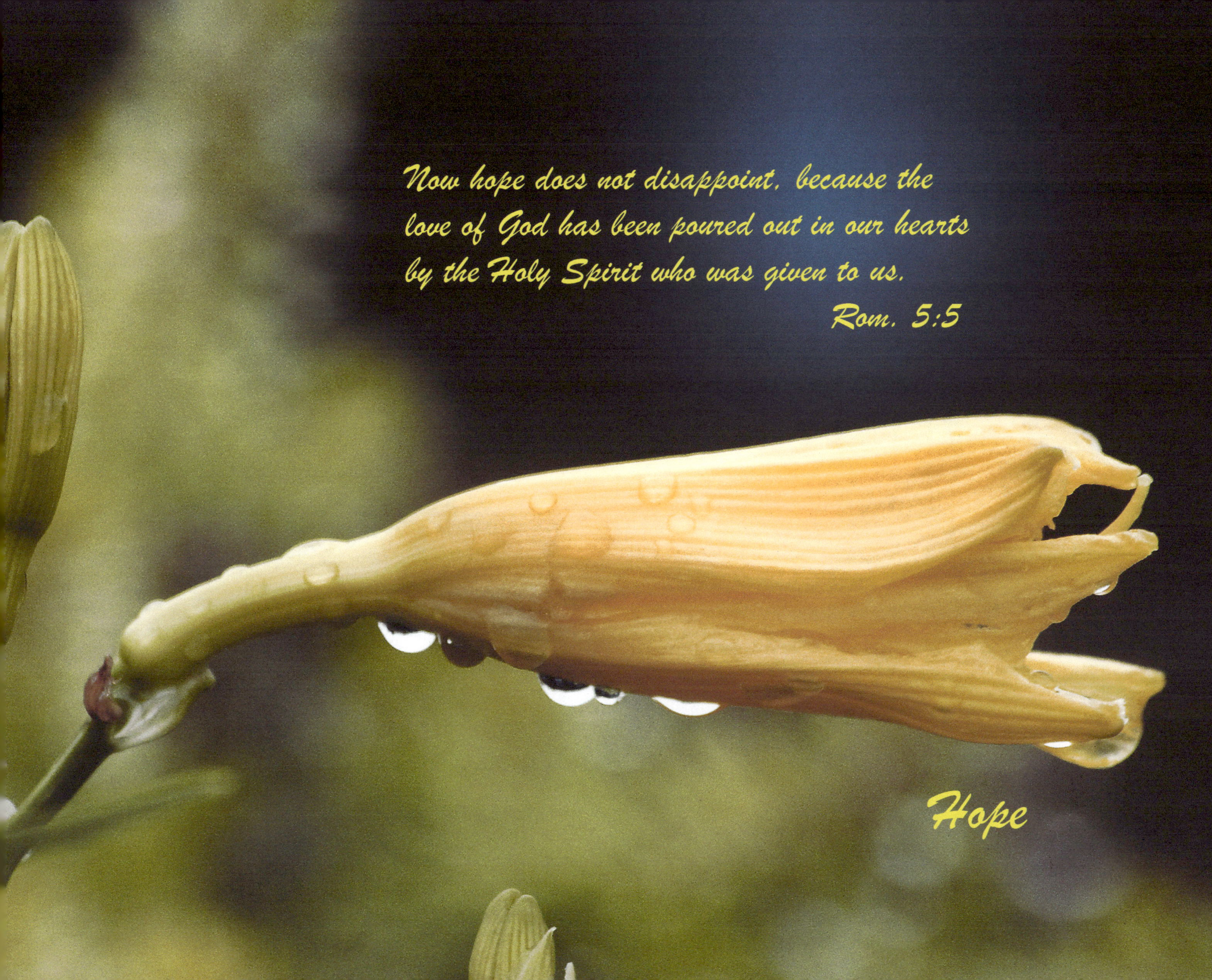
Now hope does not disappoint, because the
love of God has been poured out in our hearts
by the Holy Spirit who was given to us.
Rom. 5:5
Hope

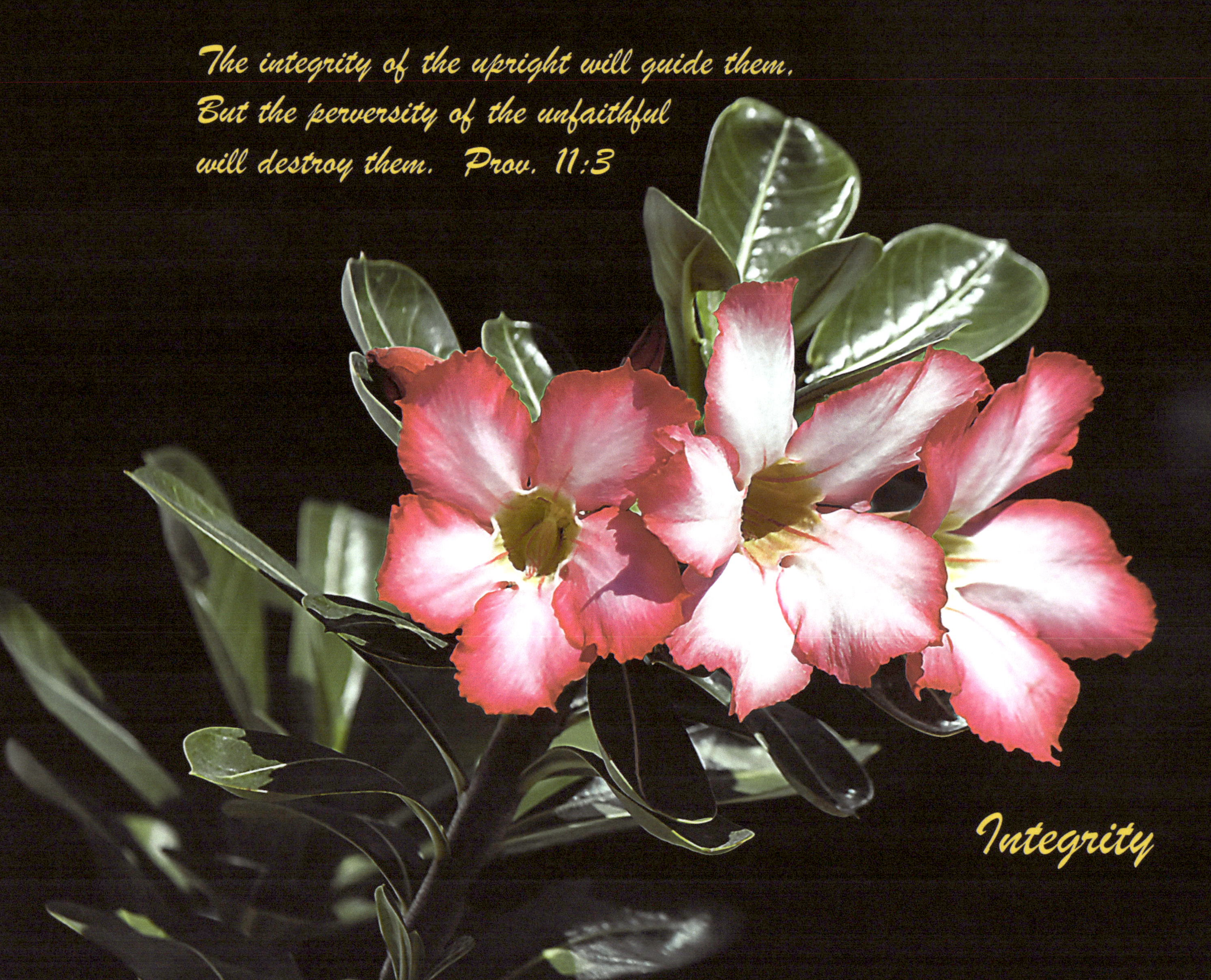
The integrity of the upright will guide them,
But the perversity of the unfaithful
will destroy them. Prov. 11:3
Integrity

Likewise the Spirit also helps in our weaknesses. For we do not know what we should pray for as we ought, but the Spirit Himself makes intercession for us with groanings which cannot be uttered. Rom. 8:26

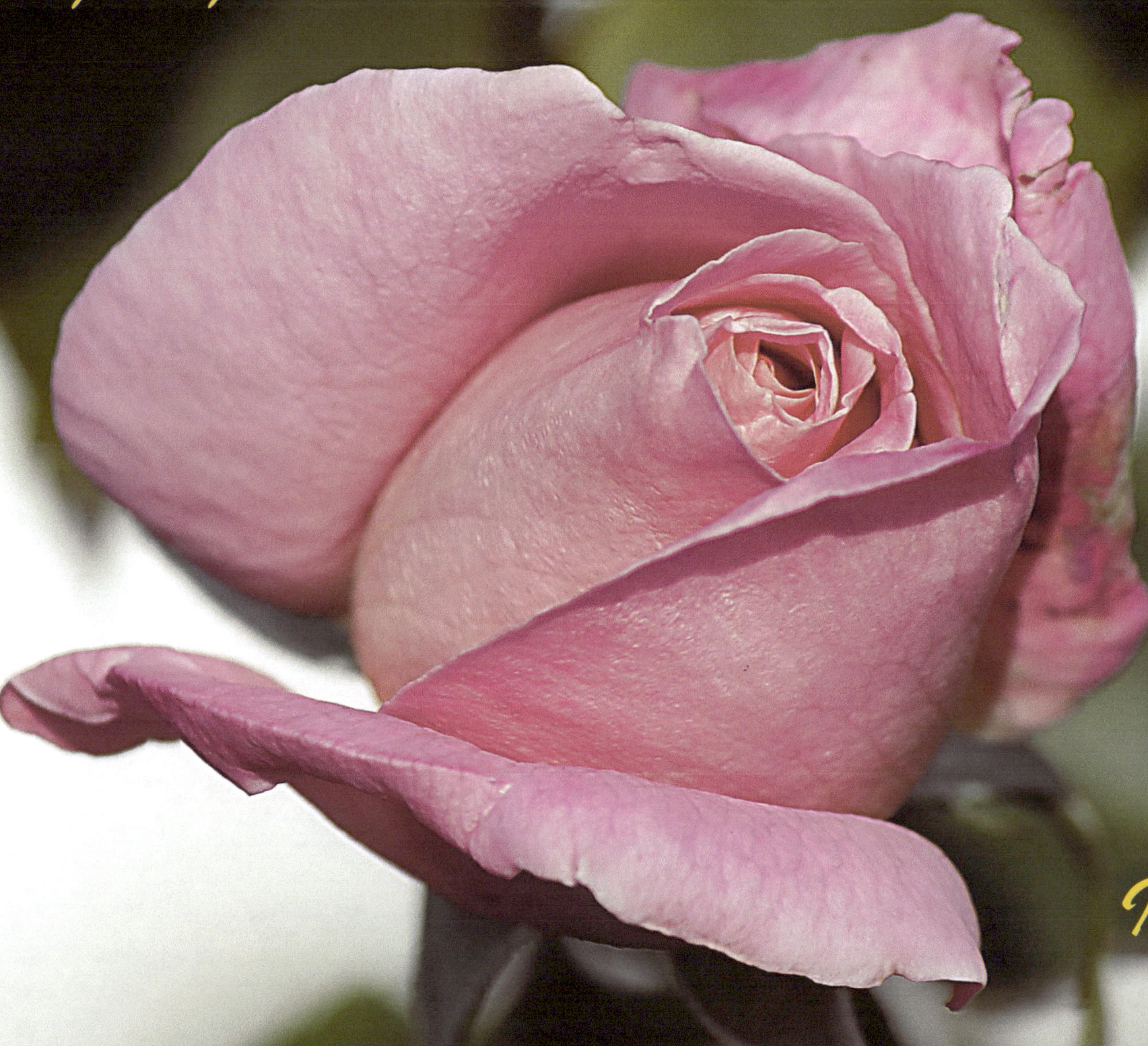

Intercession

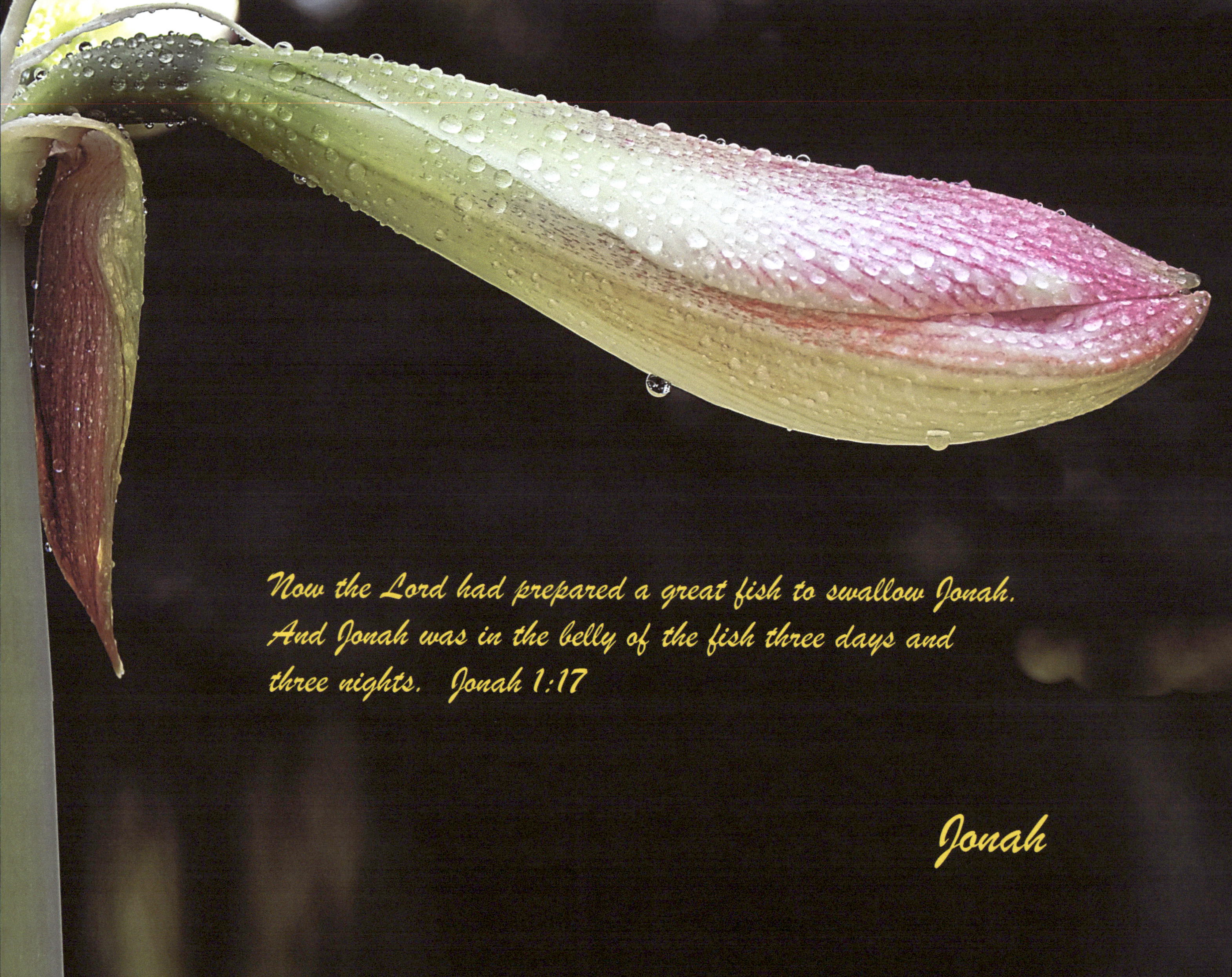
Now the Lord had prepared a great fish to swallow Jonah.
And Jonah was in the belly of the fish three days and
three nights. Jonah 1:17
Jonah

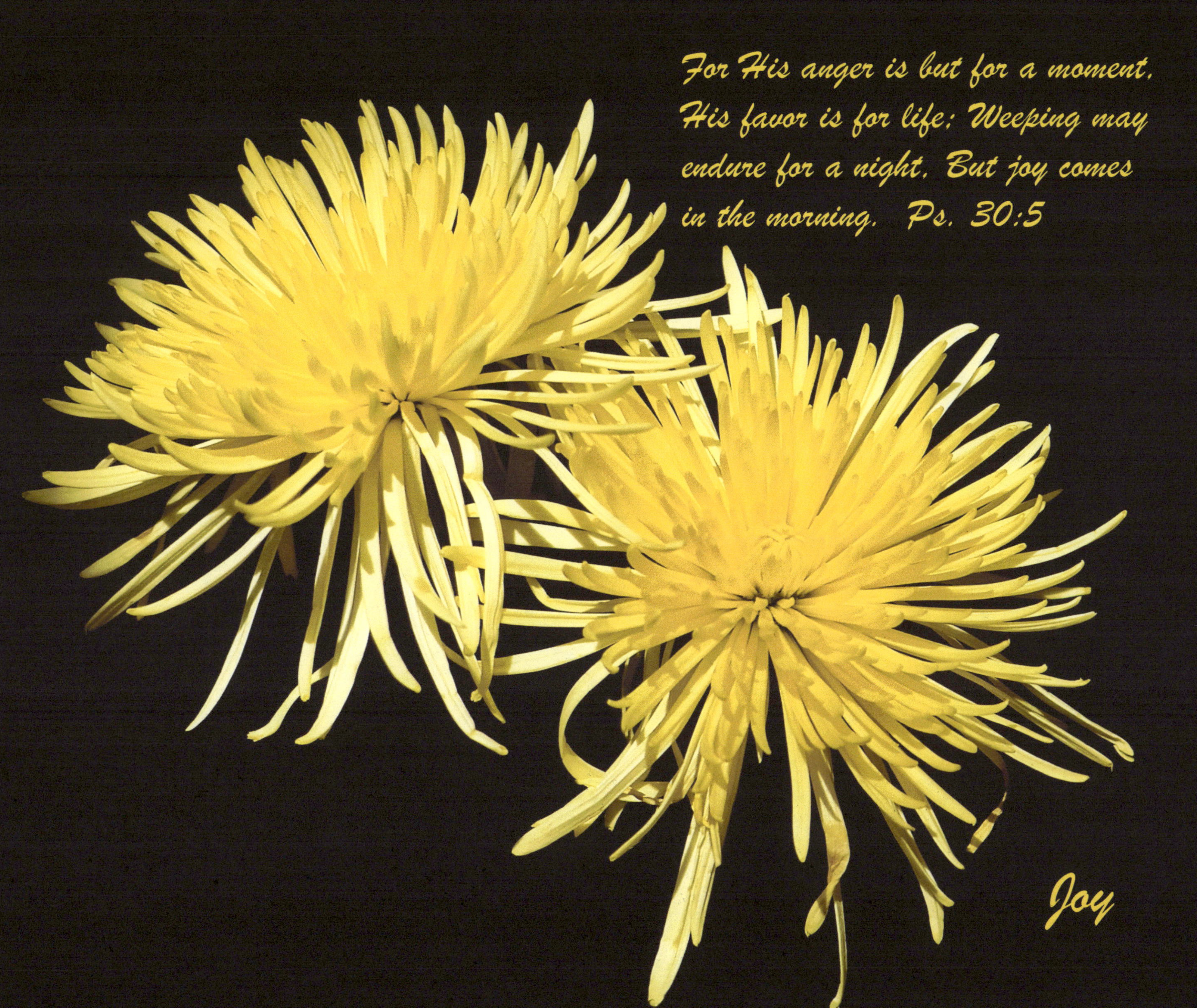
For His anger is but for a moment,
His favor is for life; Weeping may
endure for a night, But joy comes
in the morning. Ps. 30:5
Joy

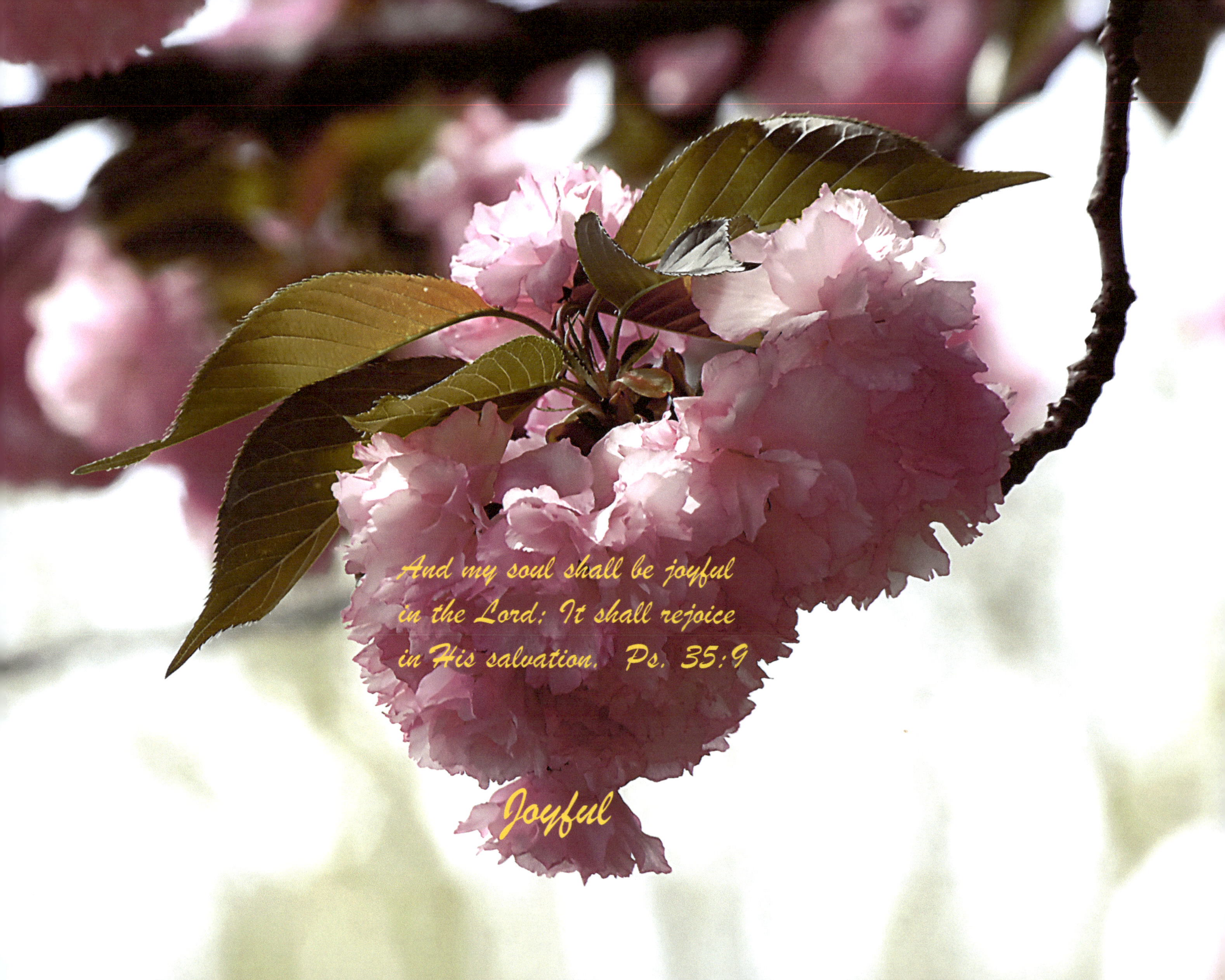
And my soul shall be joyful
in the Lord: It shall rejoice
in His salvation. Ps. 35:9
Joyful

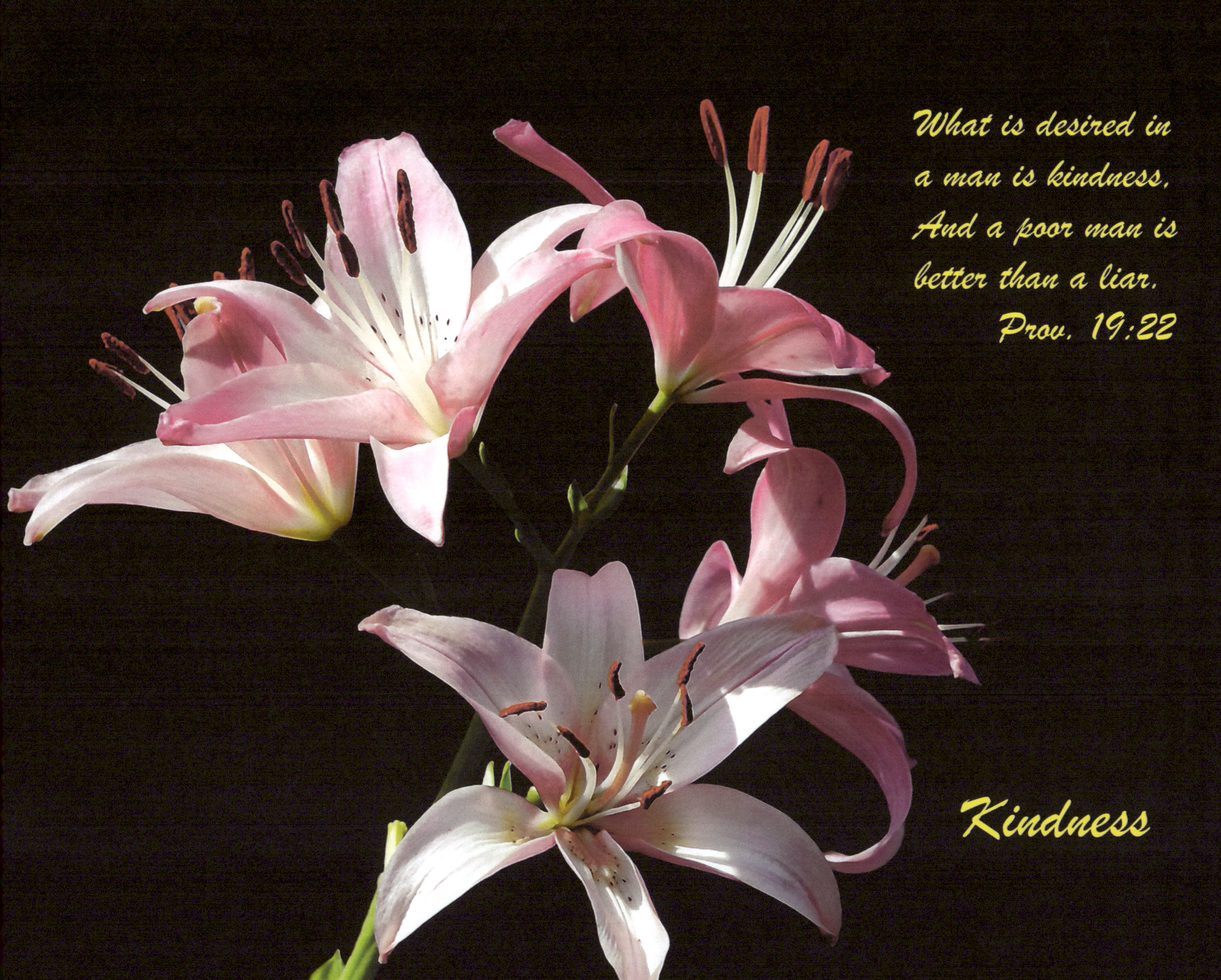
What is desired in
a man is kindness,
And a poor man is
better than a liar.
Prov. 19:22
Kindness

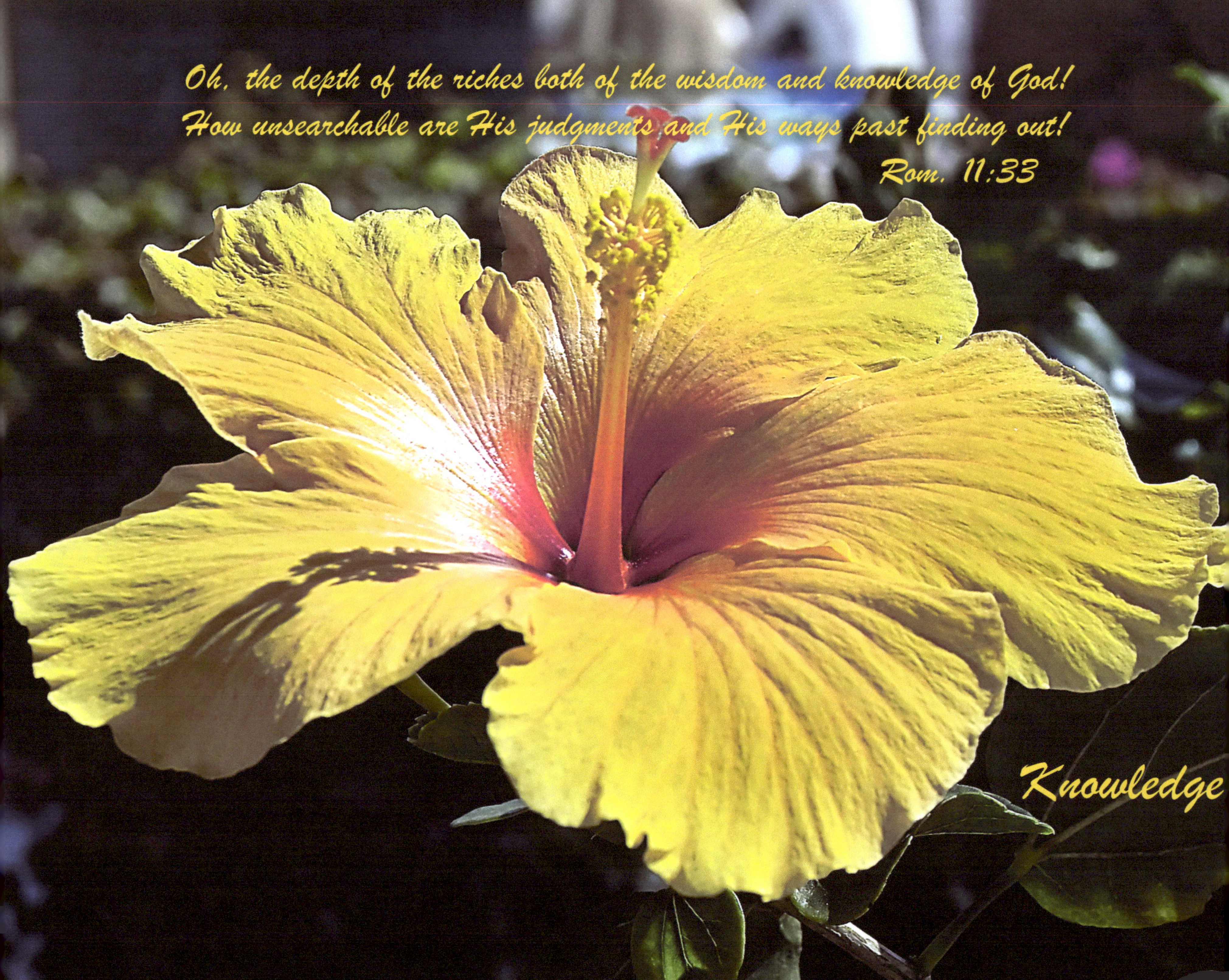
Oh, the depth of the riches both of the wisdom and knowledge of God!
How unsearchable are His judgments and His ways past finding out!
Rom. 11:33
Knowledge

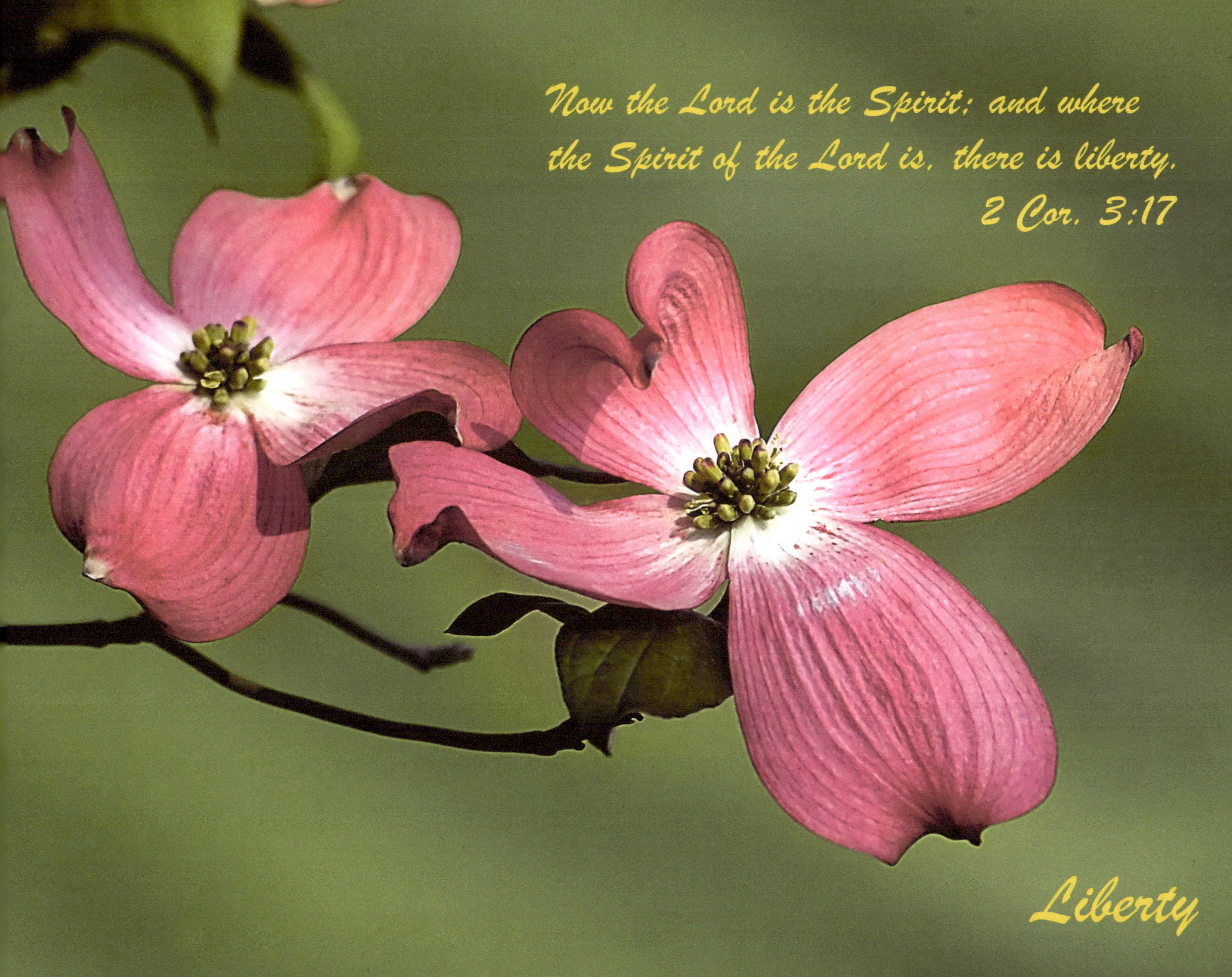
Now the Lord is the Spirit: and where
the Spirit of the Lord is, there is liberty.
2 Cor. 3:17
Liberty

Jesus said to her, "I am the resurrection and the life. He who believes in Me, though he may die, he shall live. And whoever lives and believes in Me shall never die. Do you believe this?" Jn. 11:25,26

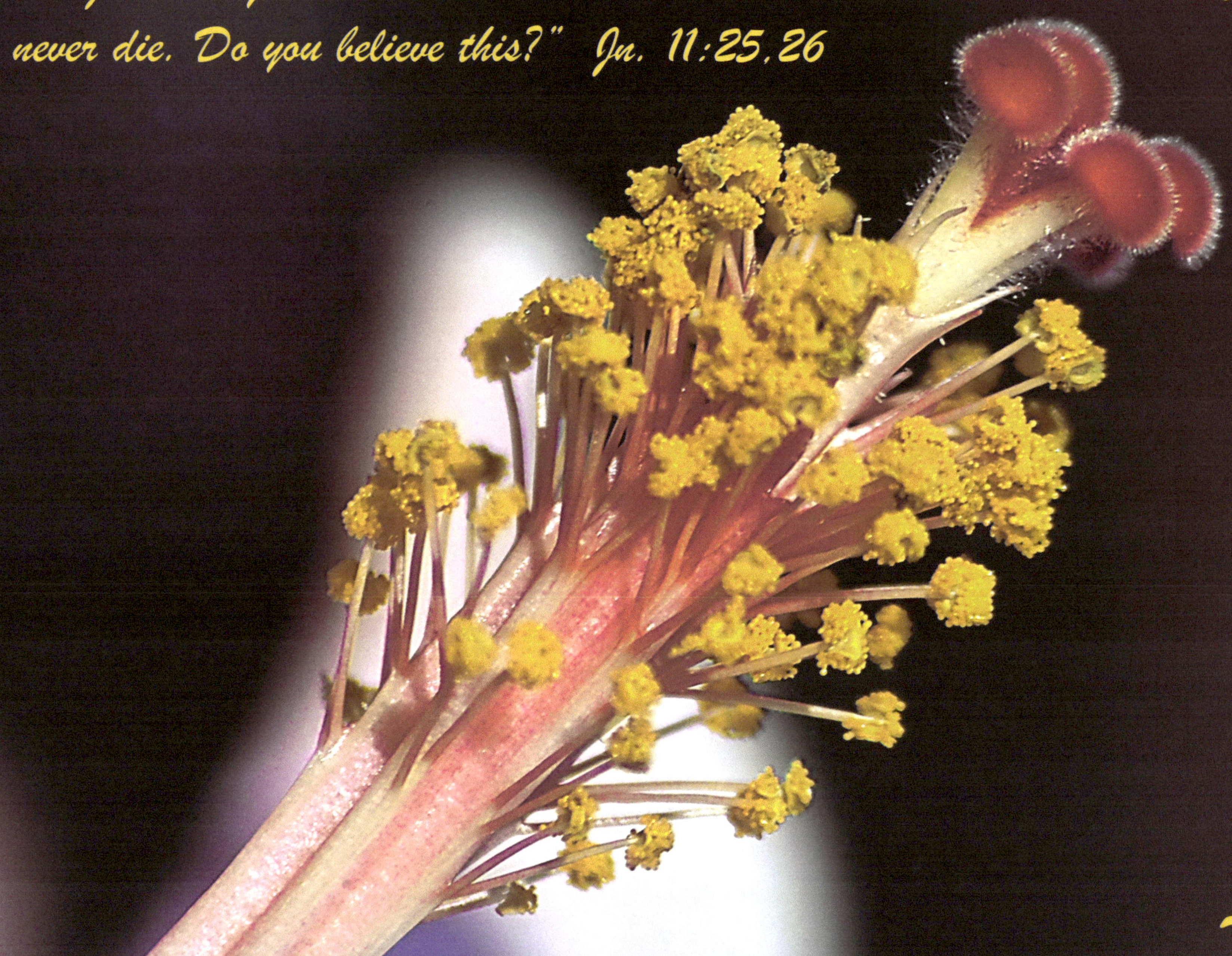

Life

Oh, that men would give thanks to the Lord for His goodness,
And for His wonderful works to the children of men! For He
satisfies the longing soul, And fills the hungry soul with goodness.

Ps. 107:8,9

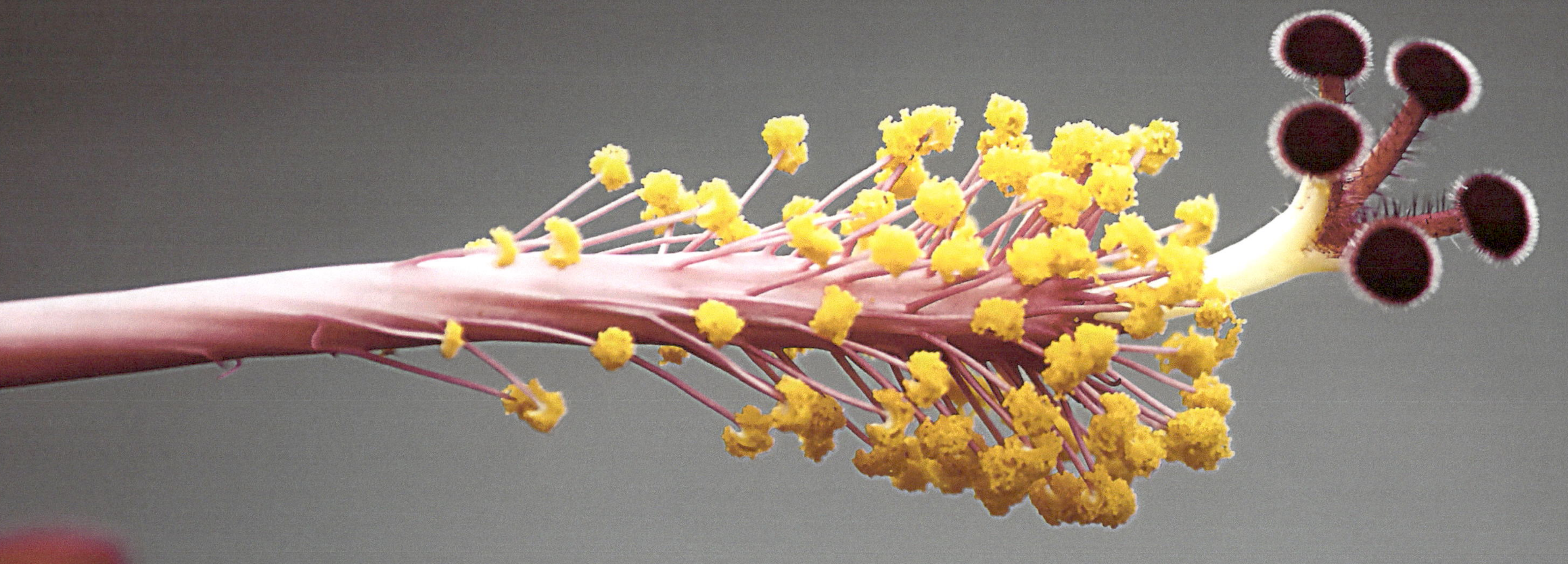

Longing

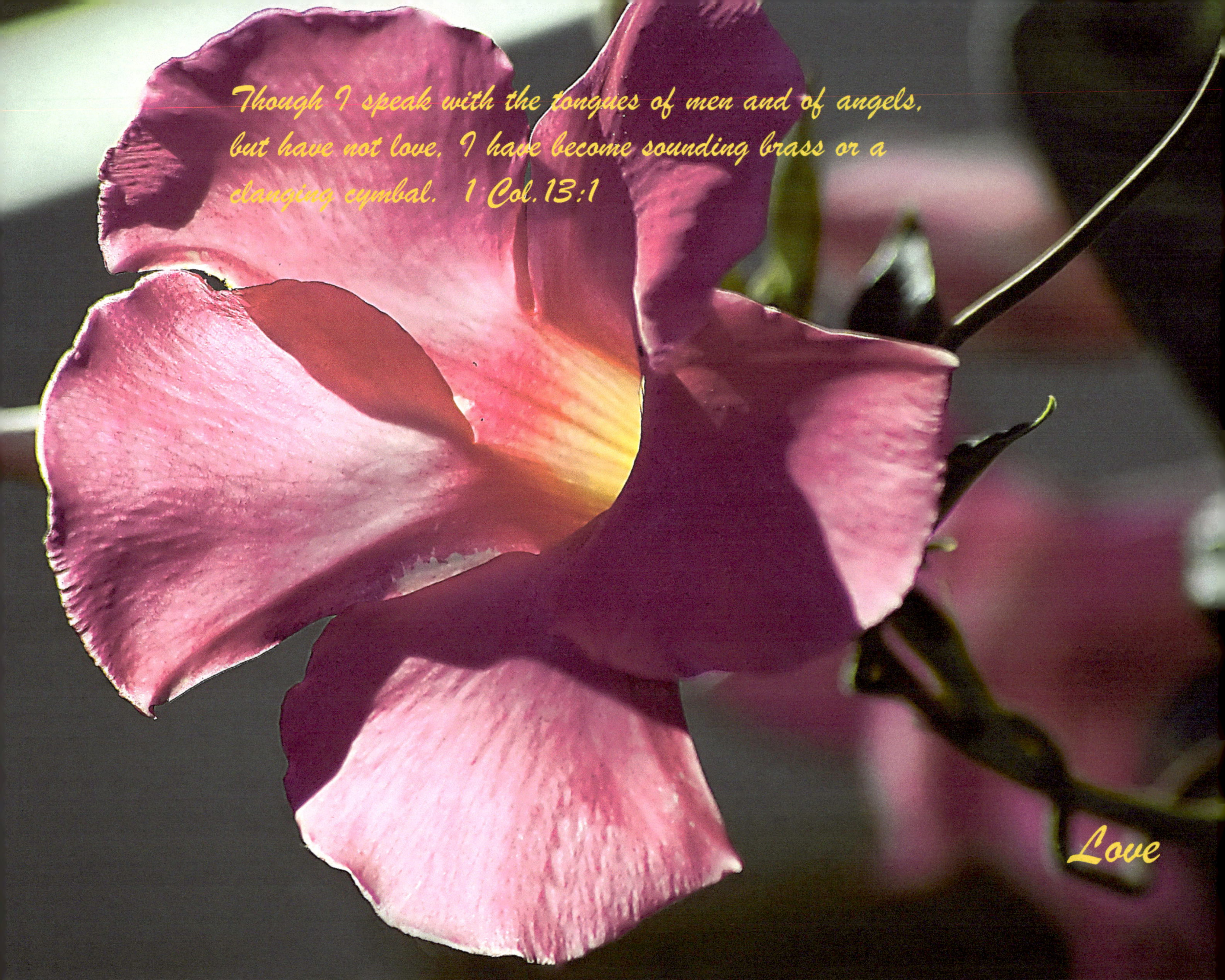
Though I speak with the tongues of men and of angels,
but have not love, I have become sounding brass or a
clanging cymbal. 1 Col.13:1
Love

Therefore, as the elect of God, holy and beloved, put on tender mercies,
kindness, humility, meekness, longsuffering; bearing with one another,
and forgiving one another, if anyone has a complaint against another;
even as Christ forgave you,
so you also must do.
Col. 3:12,13

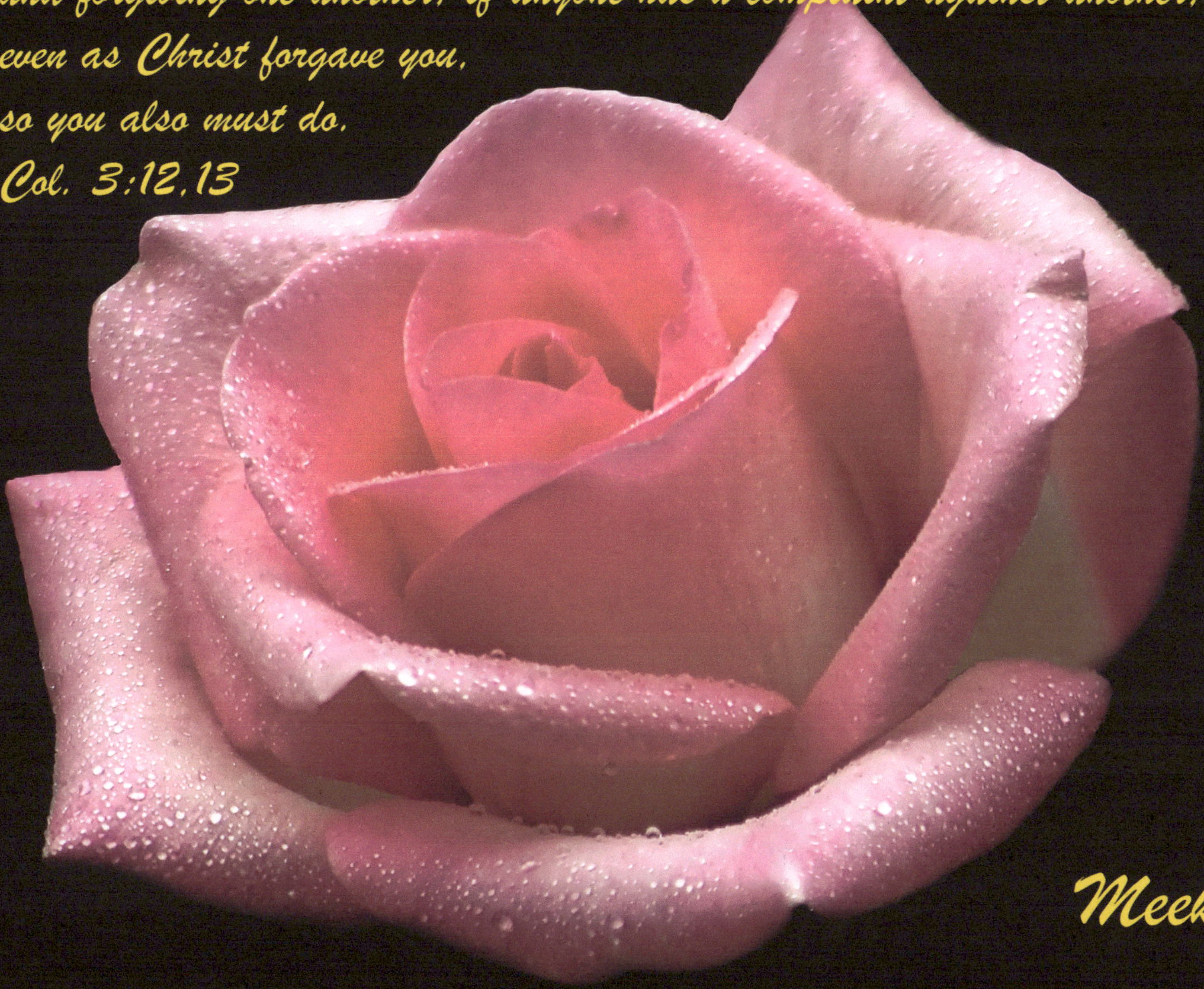

Meekness

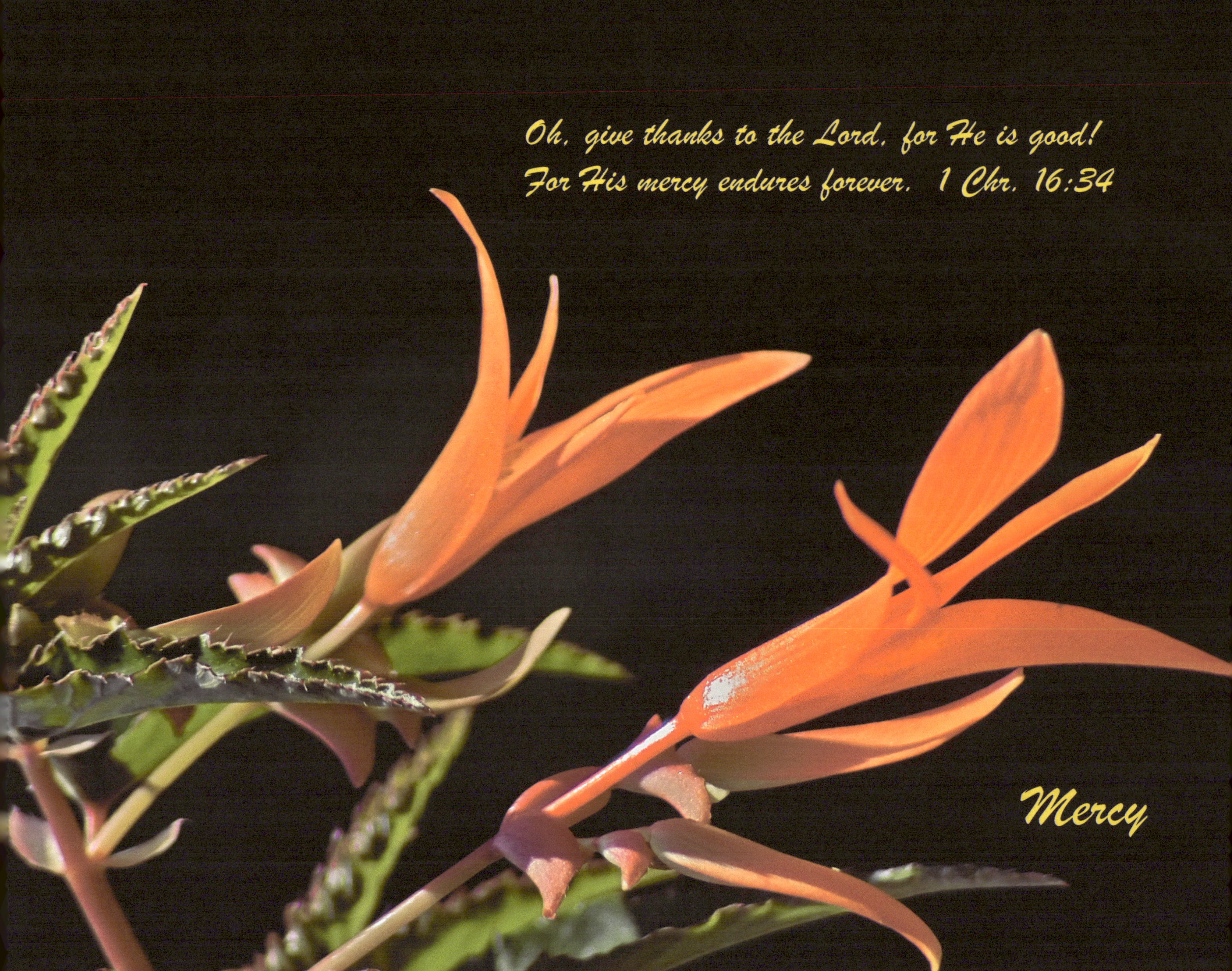
Oh, give thanks to the Lord, for He is good!
For His mercy endures forever. 1 Chr. 16:34
Mercy

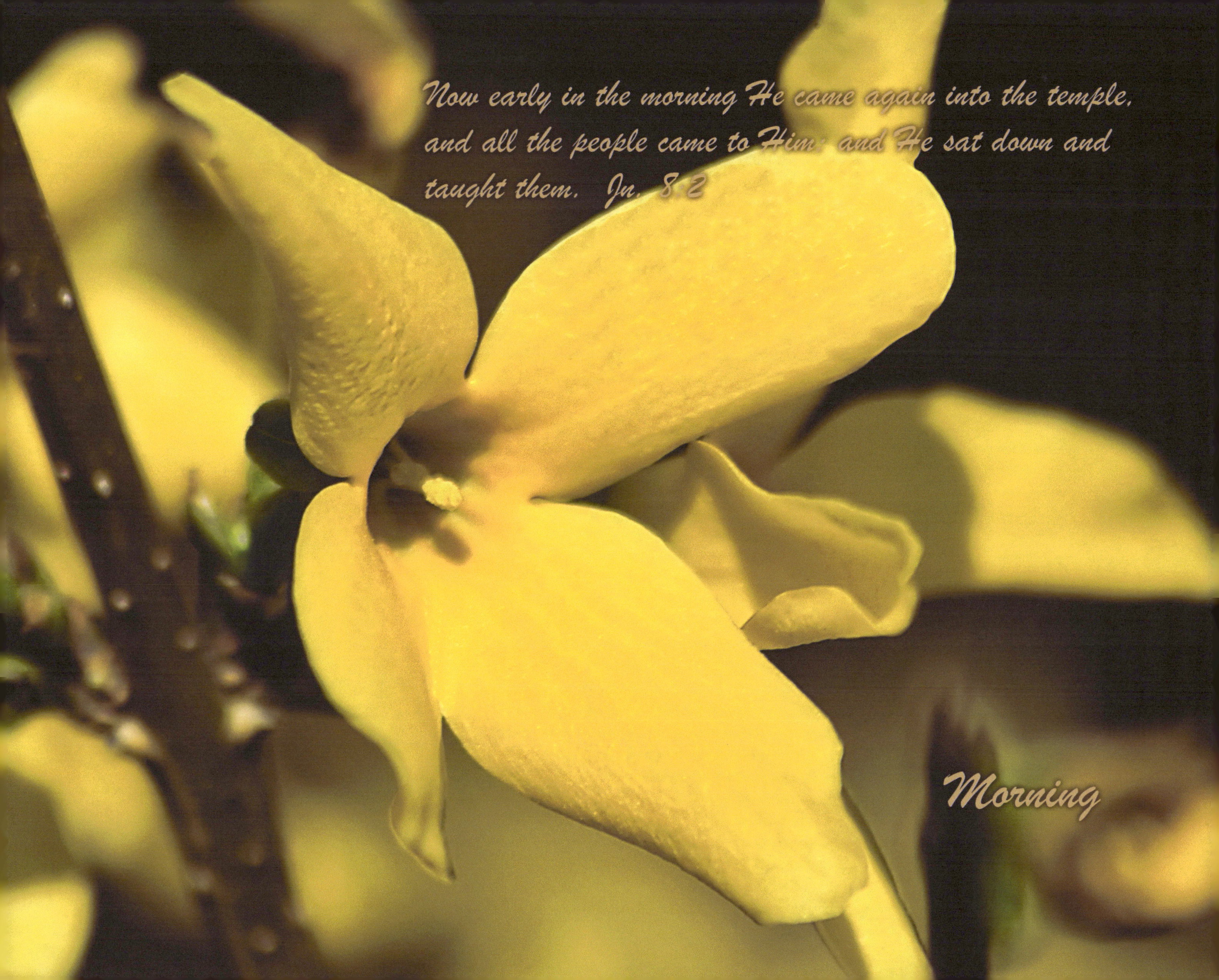

Now early in the morning He came again into the temple, and all the people came to Him; and He sat down and taught them. Jn. 8:2

Morning

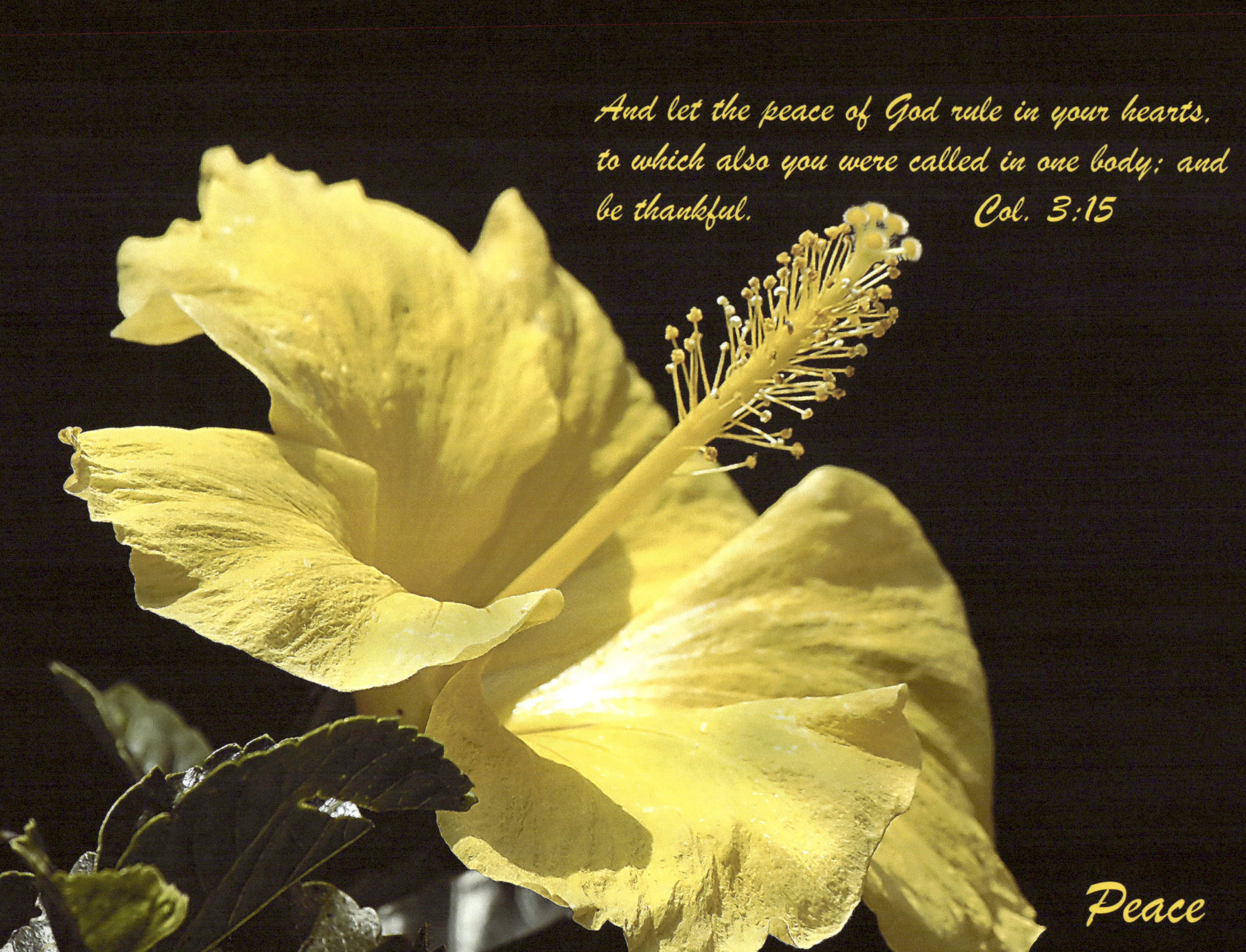
And let the peace of God rule in your hearts,
to which also you were called in one body; and
be thankful. Col. 3:15
Peace

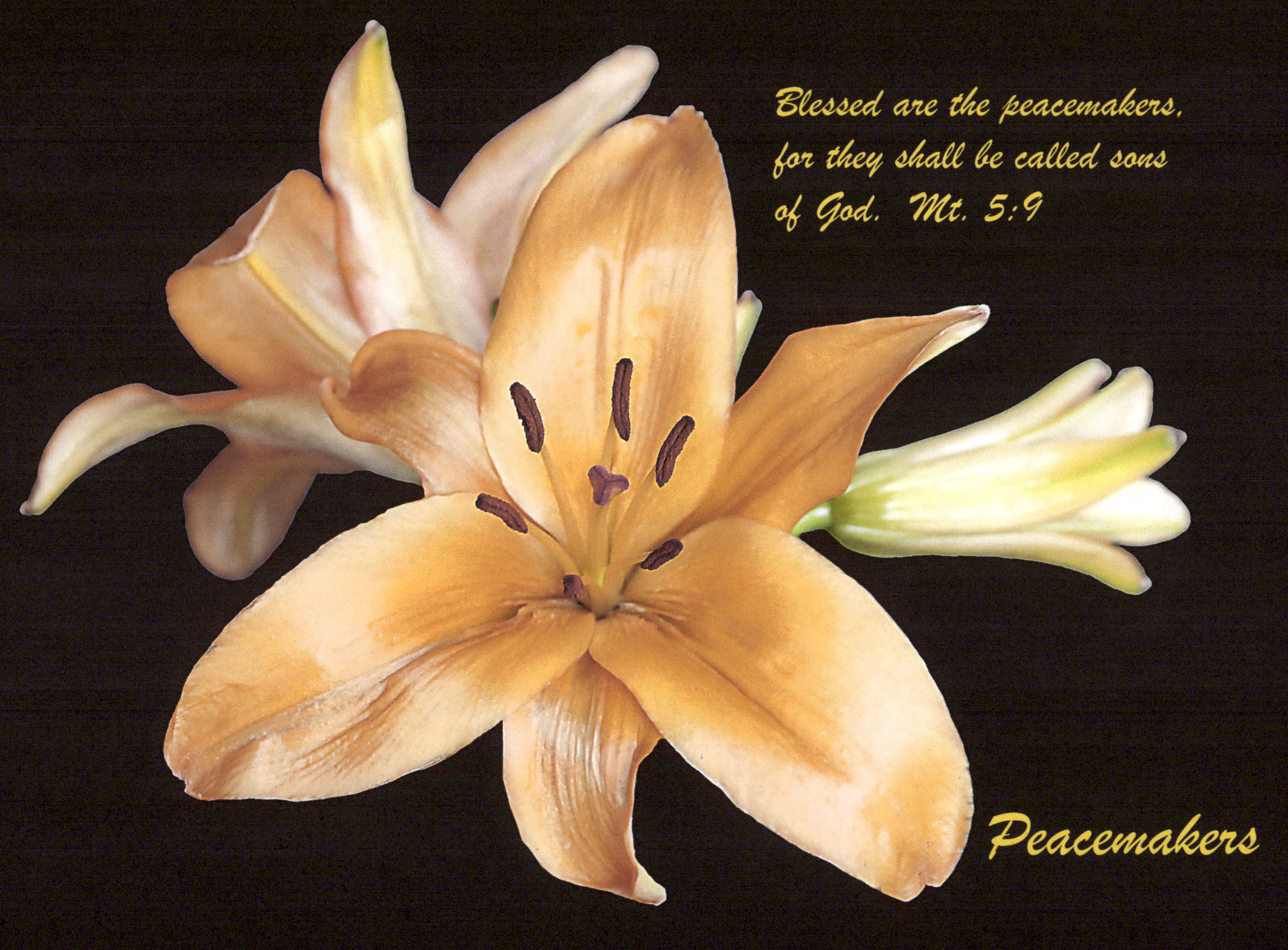
Blessed are the peacemakers,
for they shall be called sons
of God. Mt. 5:9
Peacemakers

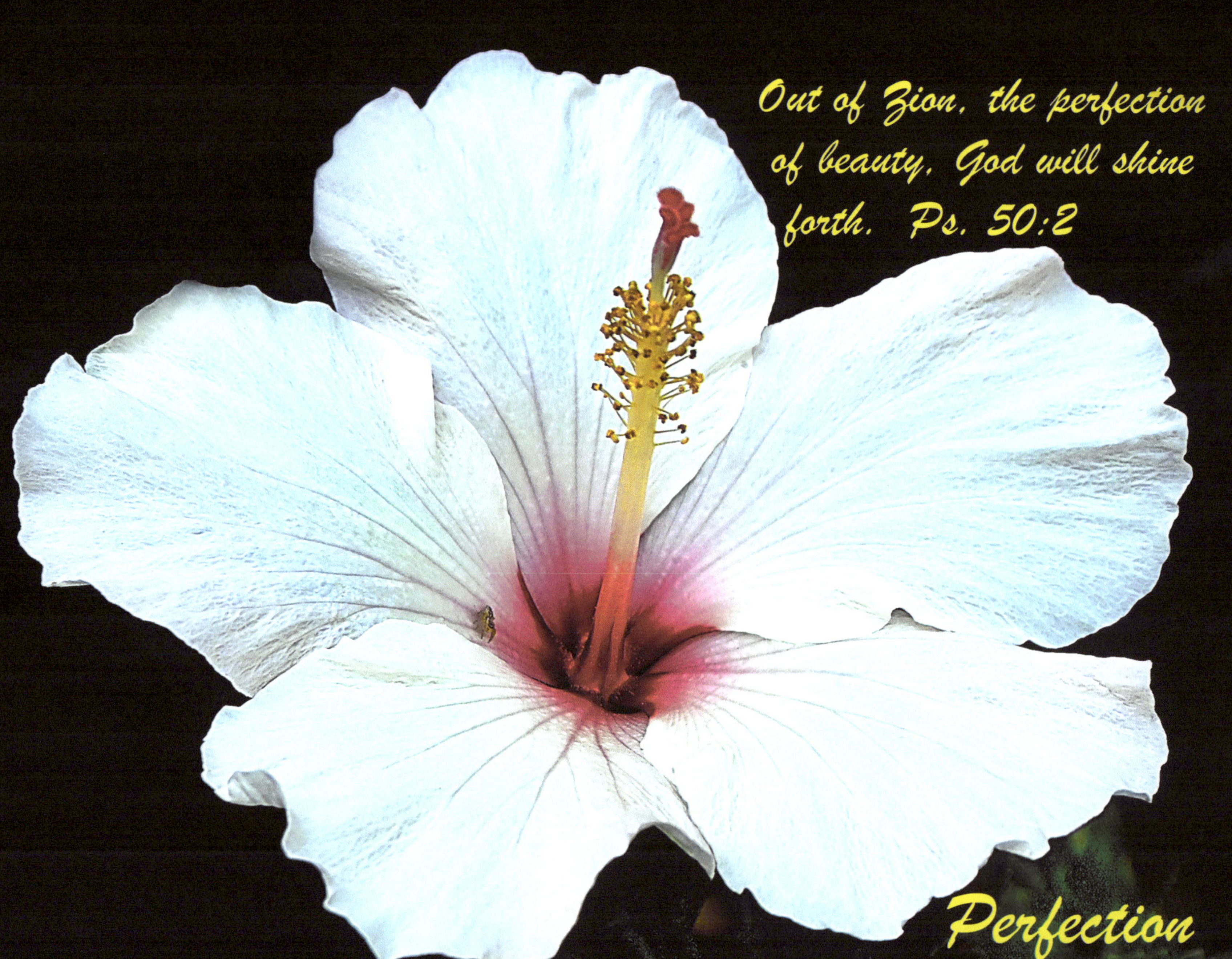
Out of Zion, the perfection
of beauty, God will shine
forth. Ps. 50:2
Perfection

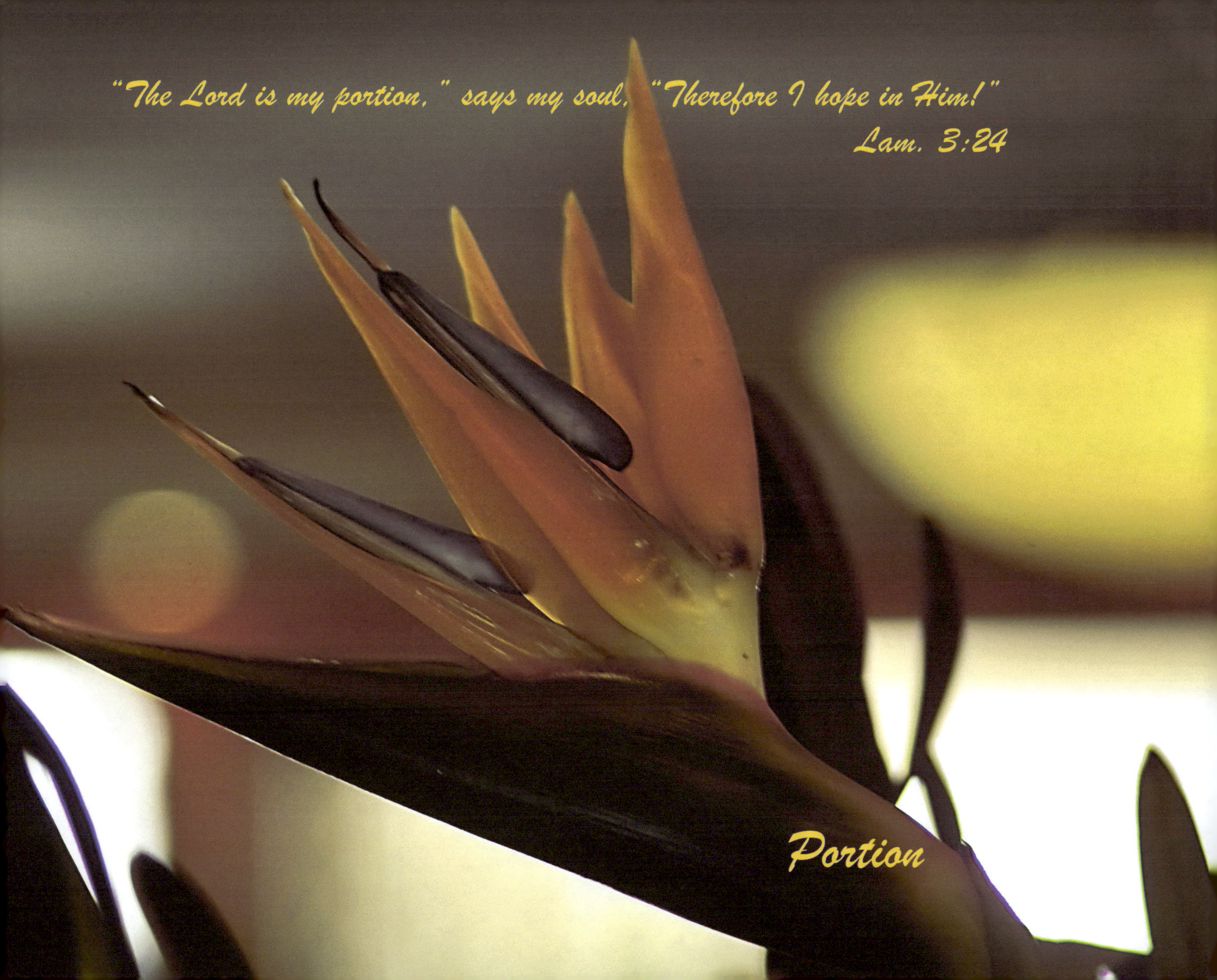

"The Lord is my portion," says my soul, "Therefore I hope in Him!"

Lam. 3:24

Portion

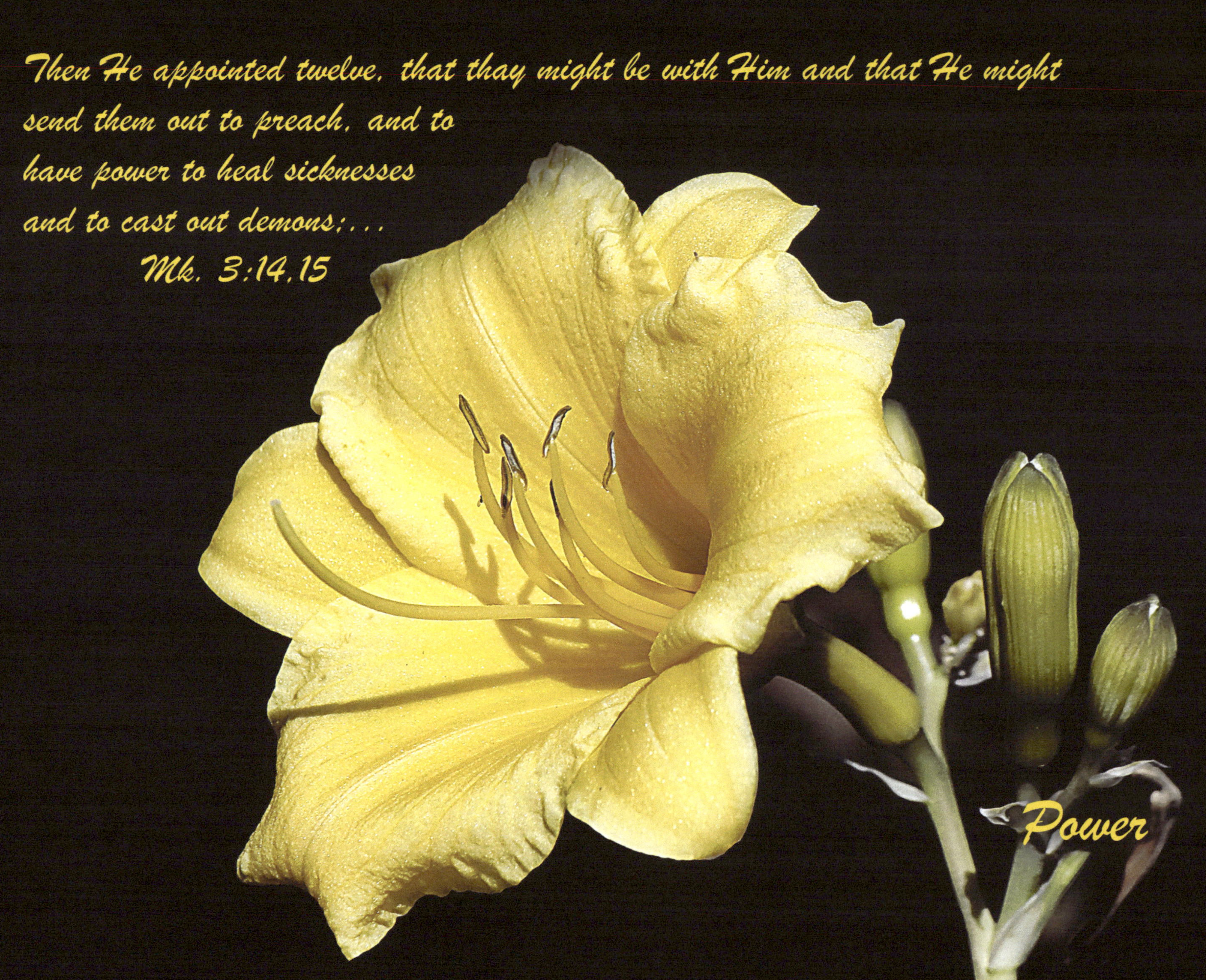
Then He appointed twelve, that thay might be with Him and that He might
send them out to preach, and to
have power to heal sicknesses
and to cast out demons;...
Mk. 3:14,15
Power

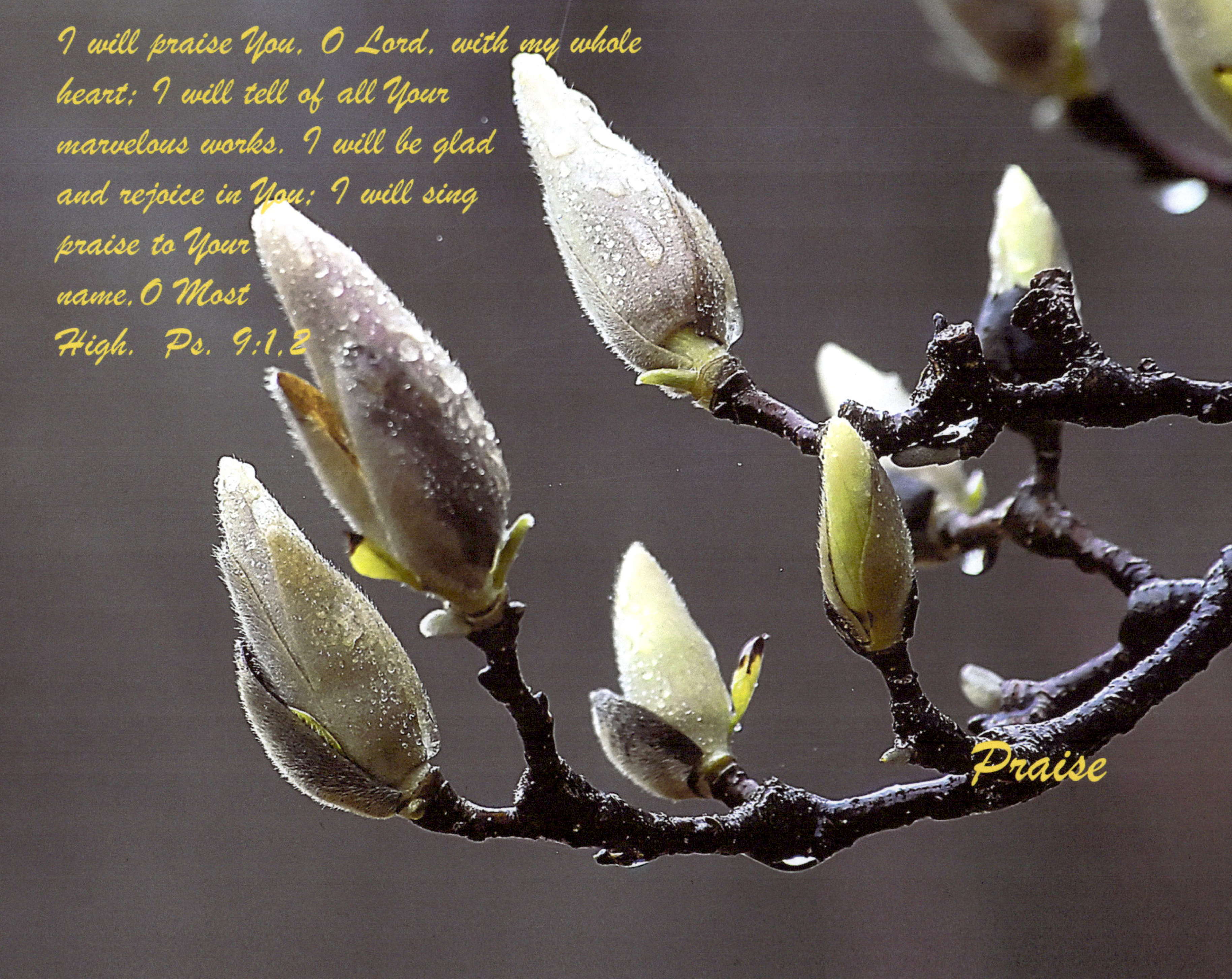
I will praise You, O Lord, with my whole
heart; I will tell of all Your
marvelous works. I will be glad
and rejoice in You; I will sing
praise to Your
name, O Most
High. Ps. 9:1,2
Praise

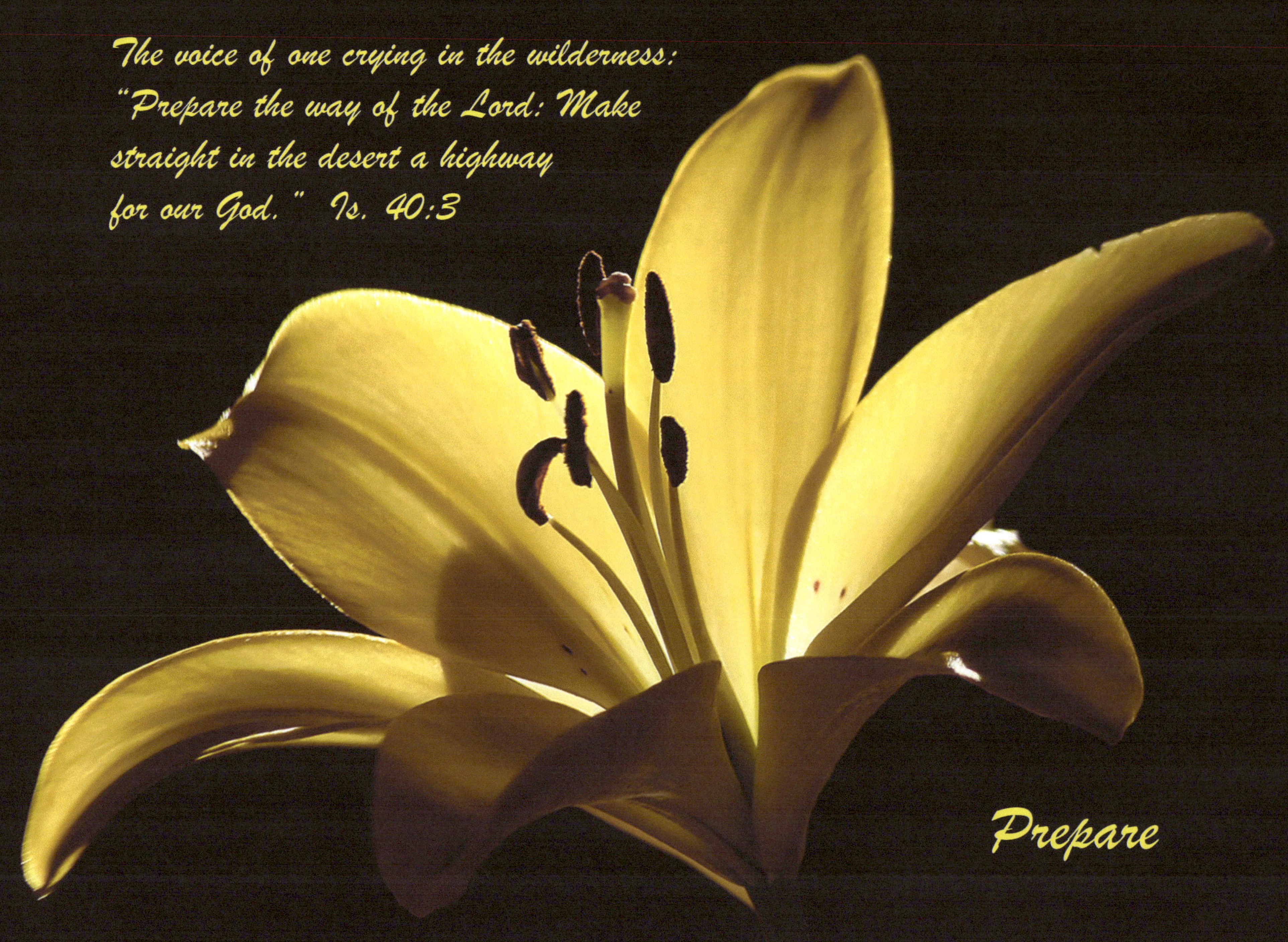
The voice of one crying in the wilderness:
"Prepare the way of the Lord: Make
straight in the desert a highway
for our God." Is. 40:3
Prepare

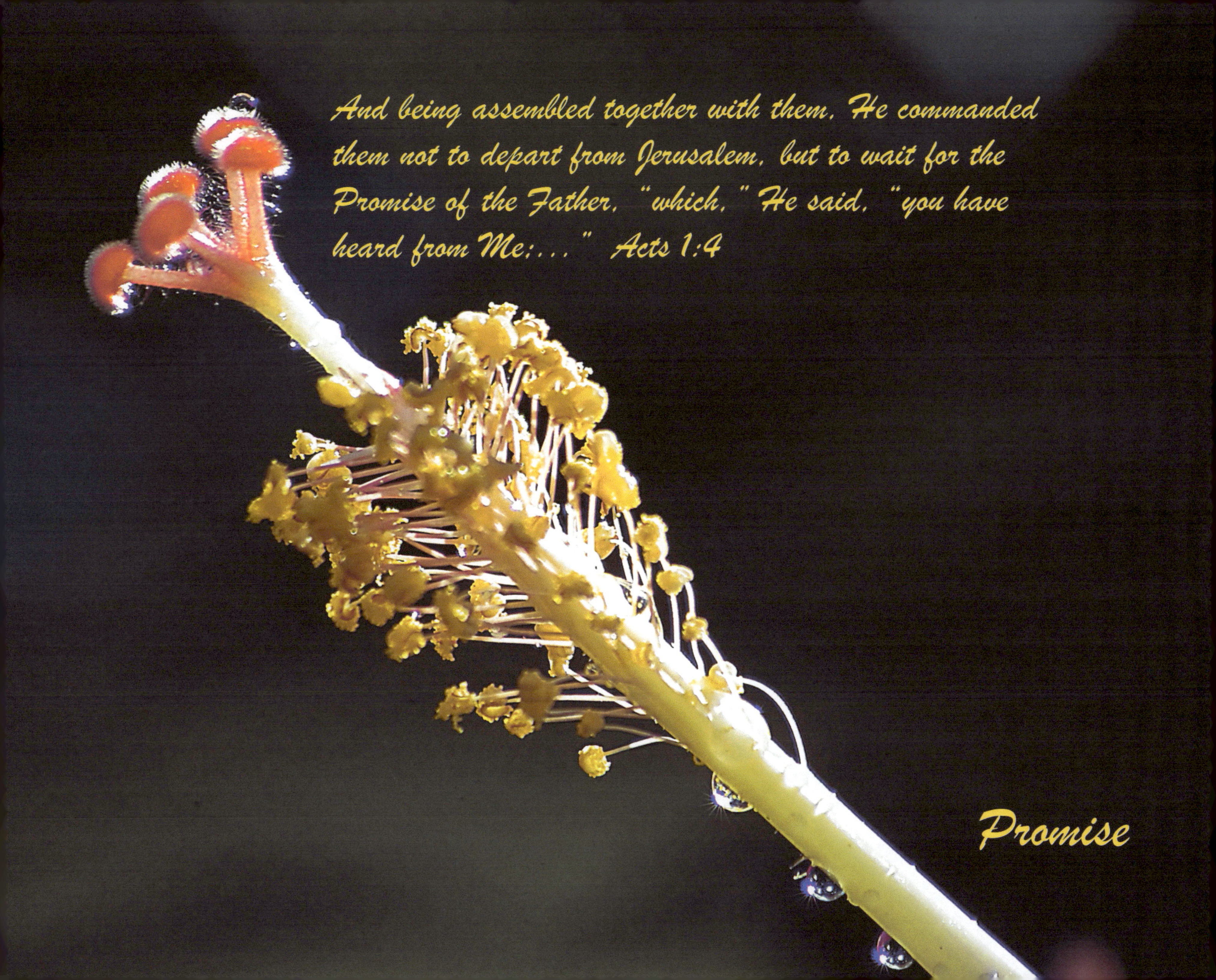

And being assembled together with them, He commanded them not to depart from Jerusalem, but to wait for the Promise of the Father, "which," He said, "you have heard from Me;. . ." Acts 1:4

Promise

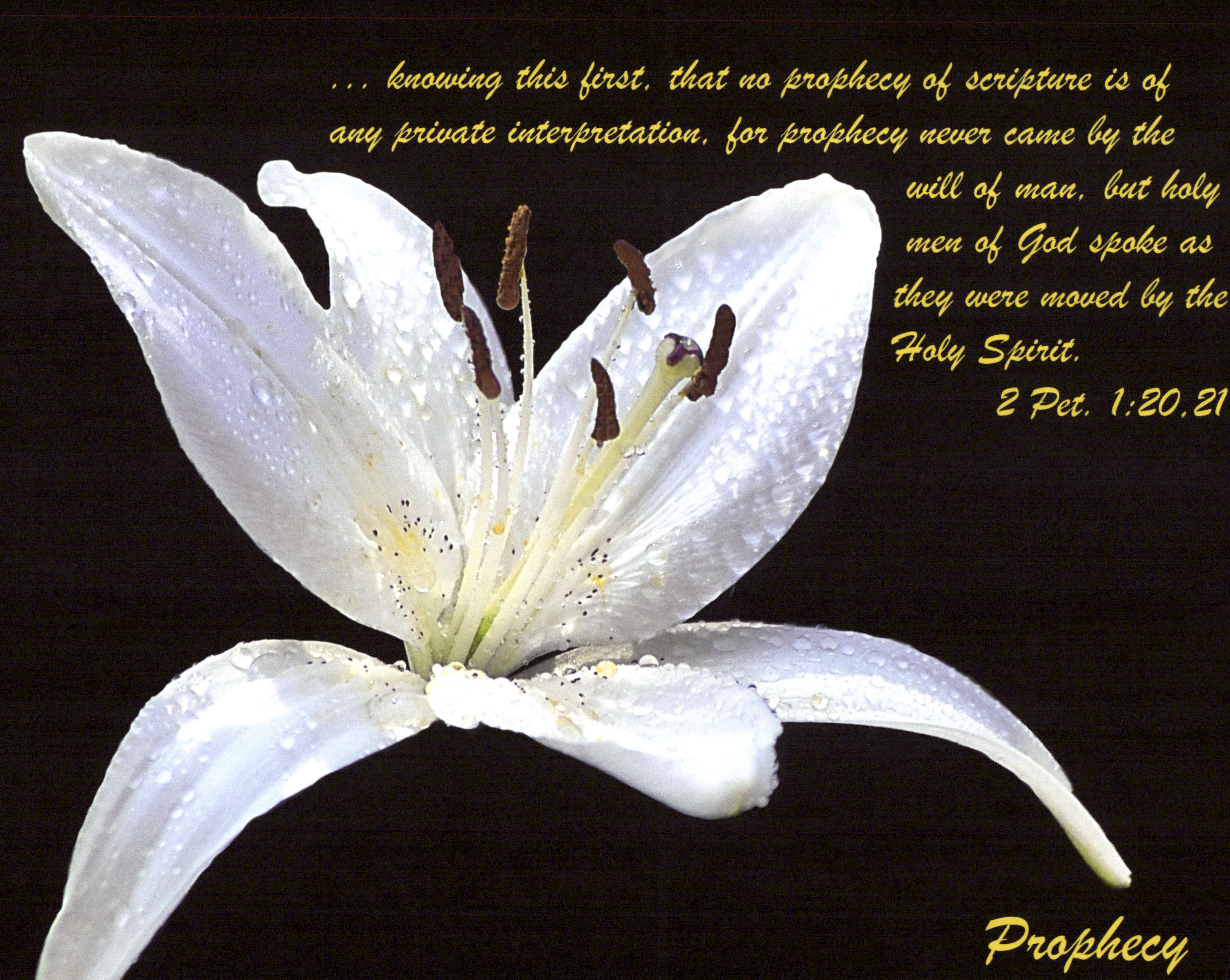
… knowing this first, that no prophecy of scripture is of
any private interpretation, for prophecy never came by the
will of man, but holy
men of God spoke as
they were moved by the
Holy Spirit.
2 Pet. 1:20,21
Prophecy

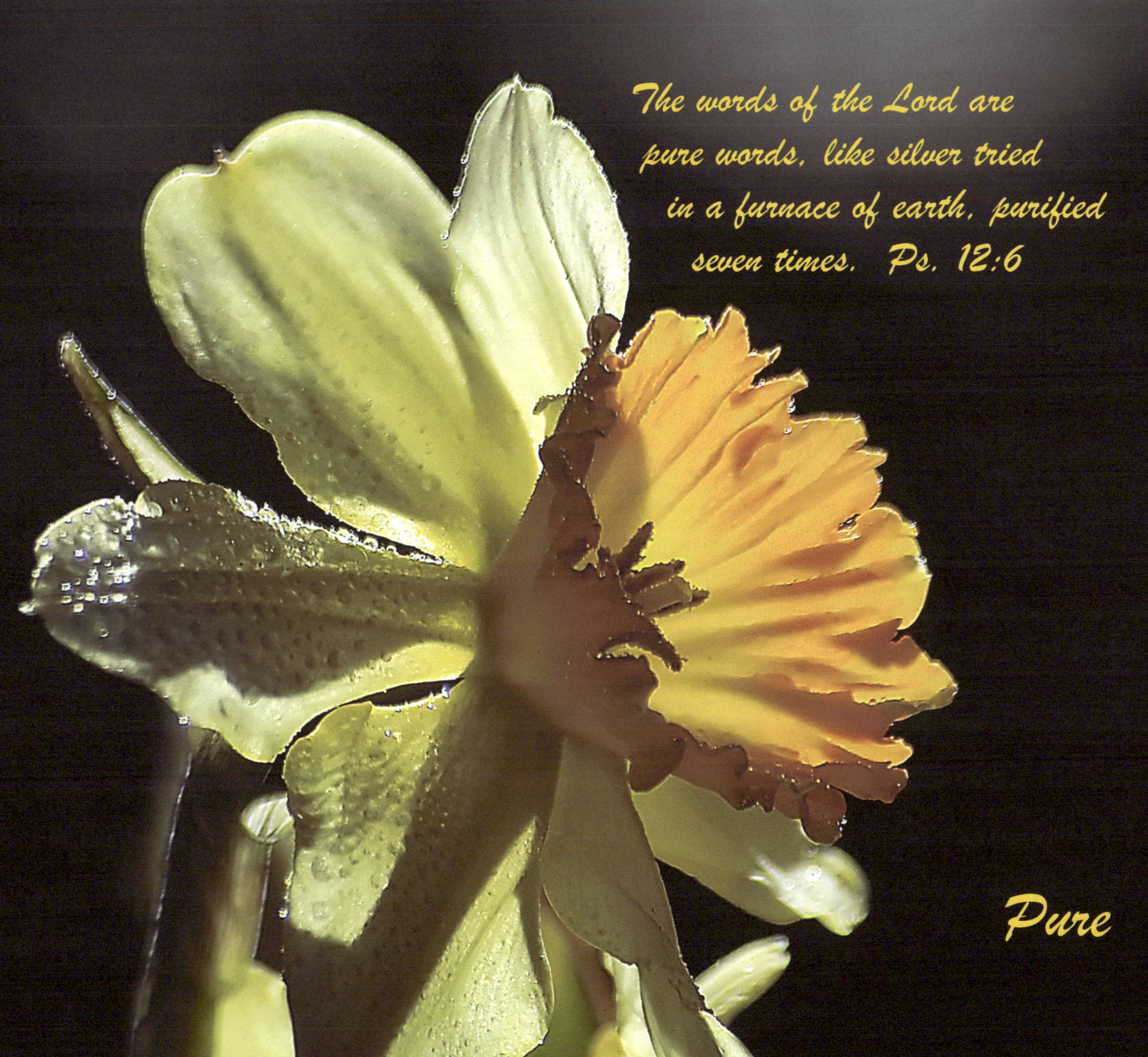
The words of the Lord are
pure words, like silver tried
in a furnace of earth, purified
seven times. Ps. 12:6
Pure

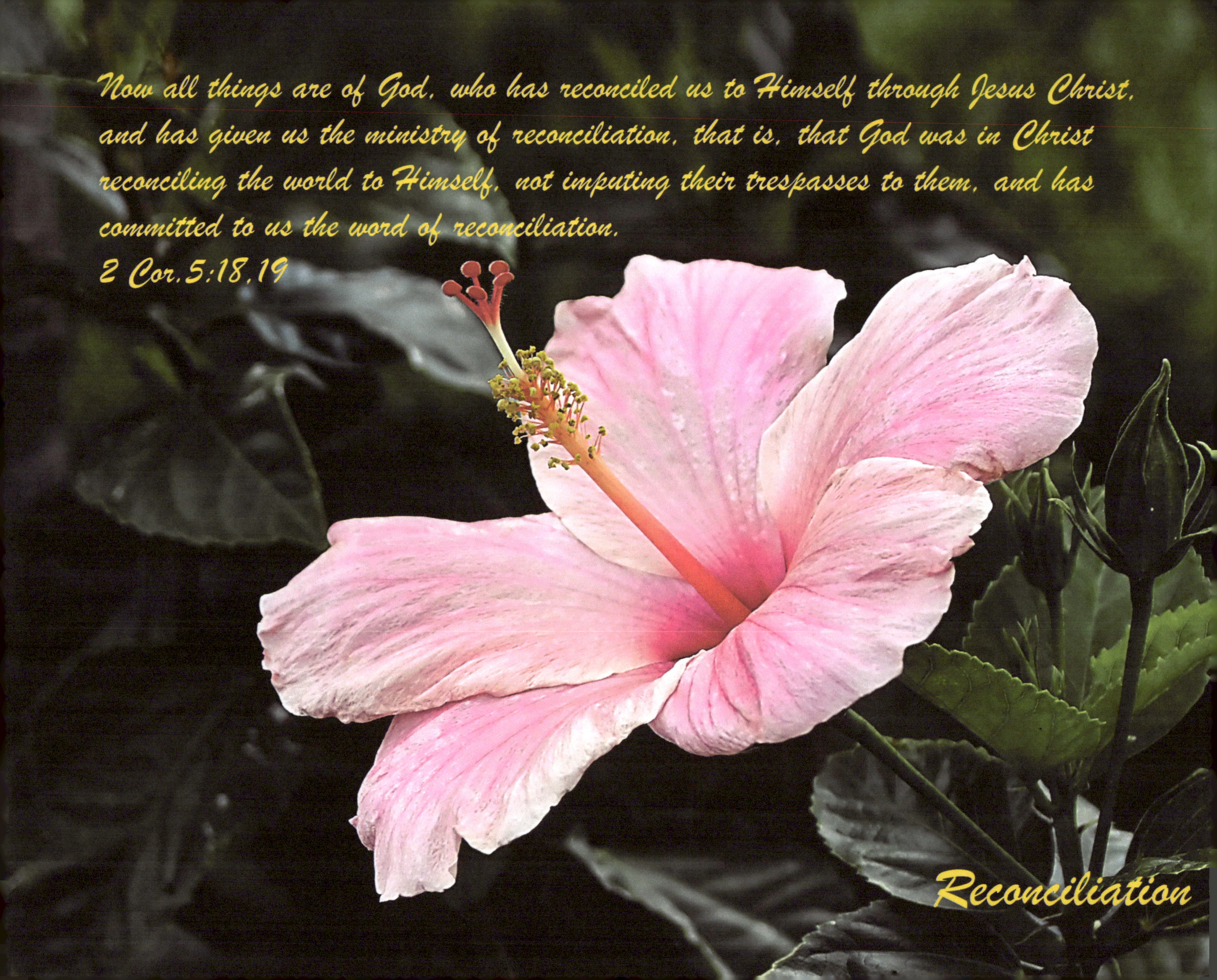

Now all things are of God, who has reconciled us to Himself through Jesus Christ, and has given us the ministry of reconciliation, that is, that God was in Christ reconciling the world to Himself, not imputing their trespasses to them, and has committed to us the word of reconciliation.

2 Cor. 5:18, 19

Reconciliation

Christ has redeemed us from the curse of the law, having become a curse for us (for it is written, "Cursed is everyone who hangs on a tree"), that the blessing of Abraham might come upon the Gentiles in Christ Jesus, that we might receive the promise of the Spirit through faith. Gal. 3:13,14

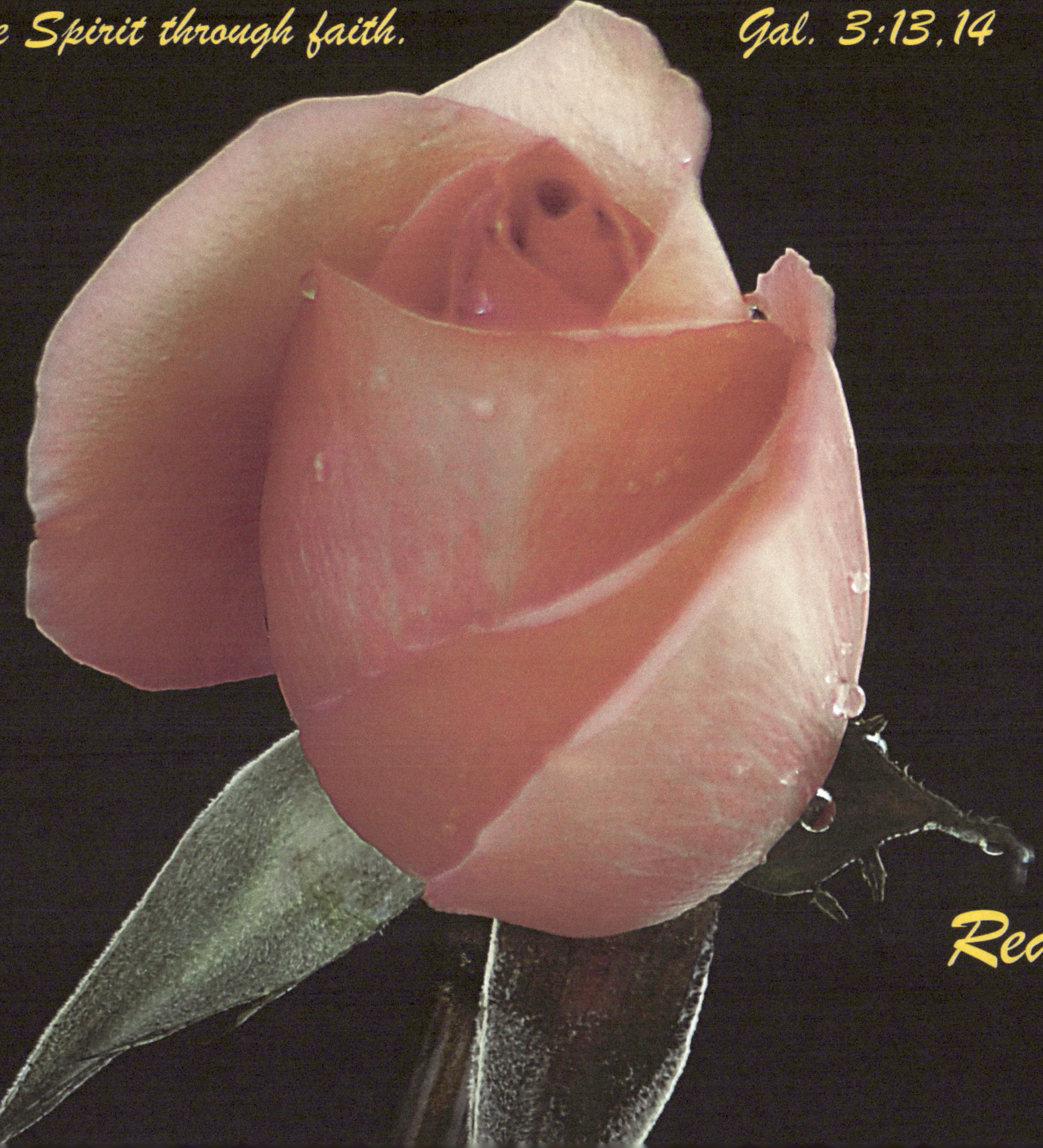

Redeemed

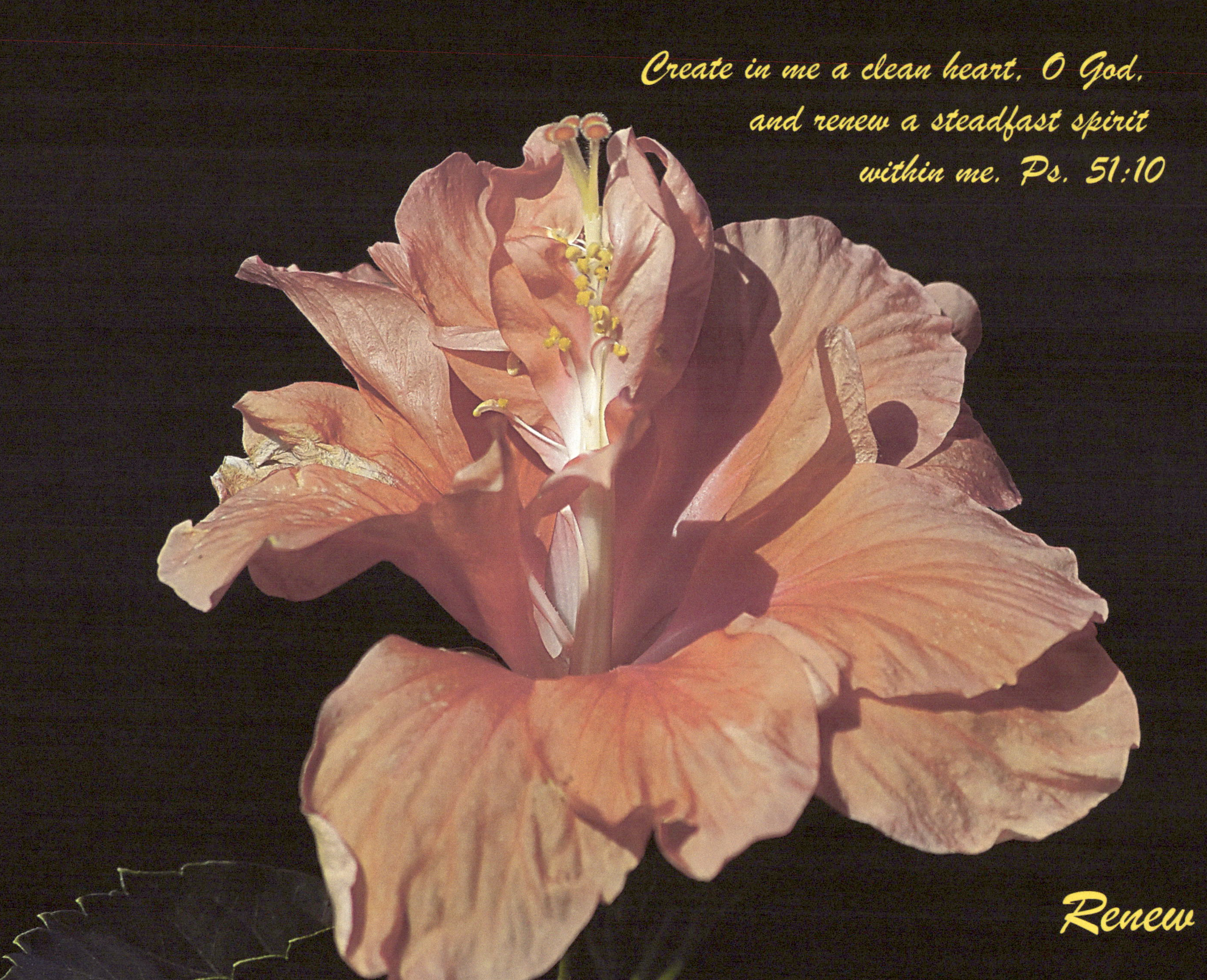
Create in me a clean heart, O God,
and renew a steadfast spirit
within me. Ps. 51:10
Renew

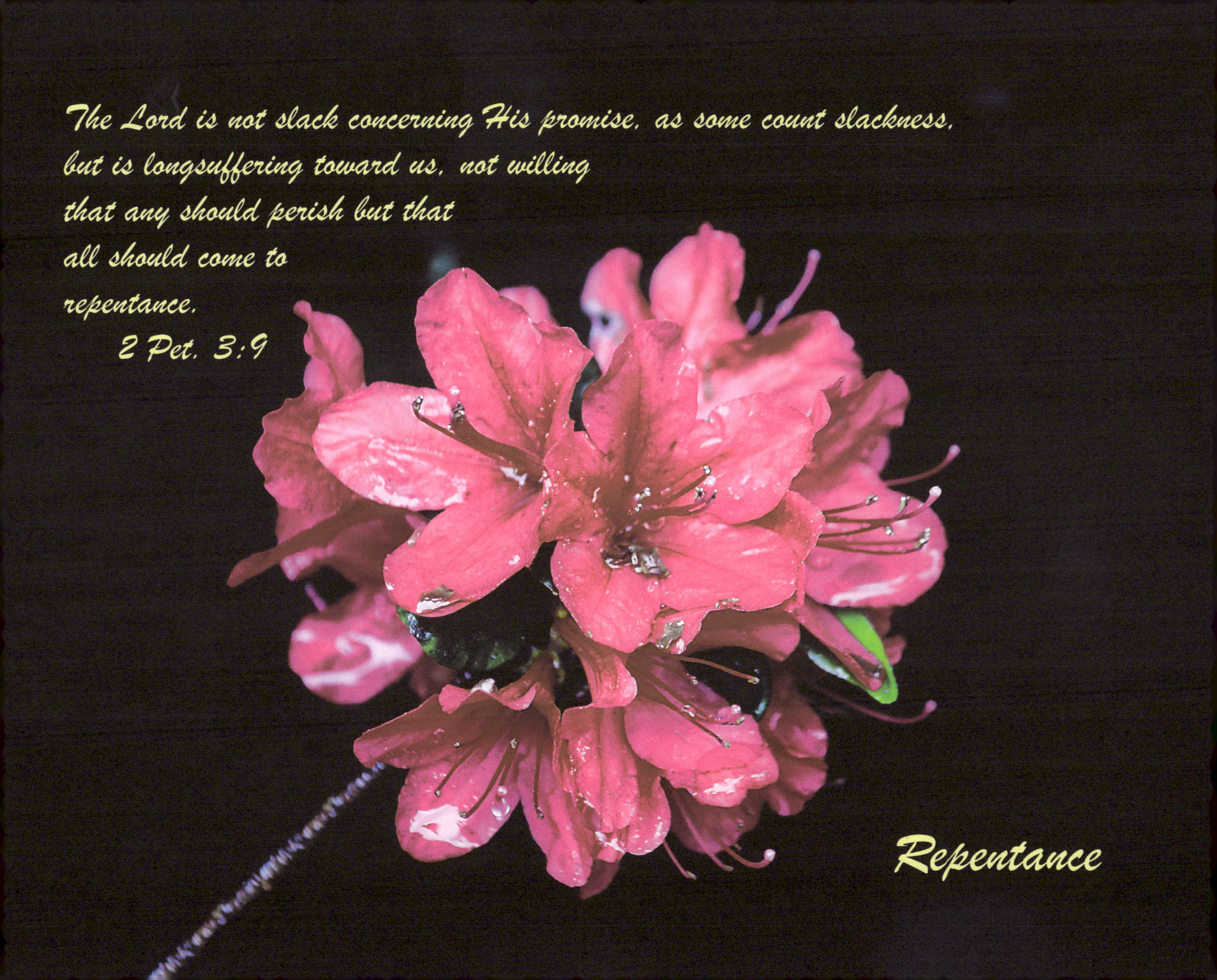

The Lord is not slack concerning His promise, as some count slackness, but is longsuffering toward us, not willing that any should perish but that all should come to repentance.

2 Pet. 3:9

Repentance

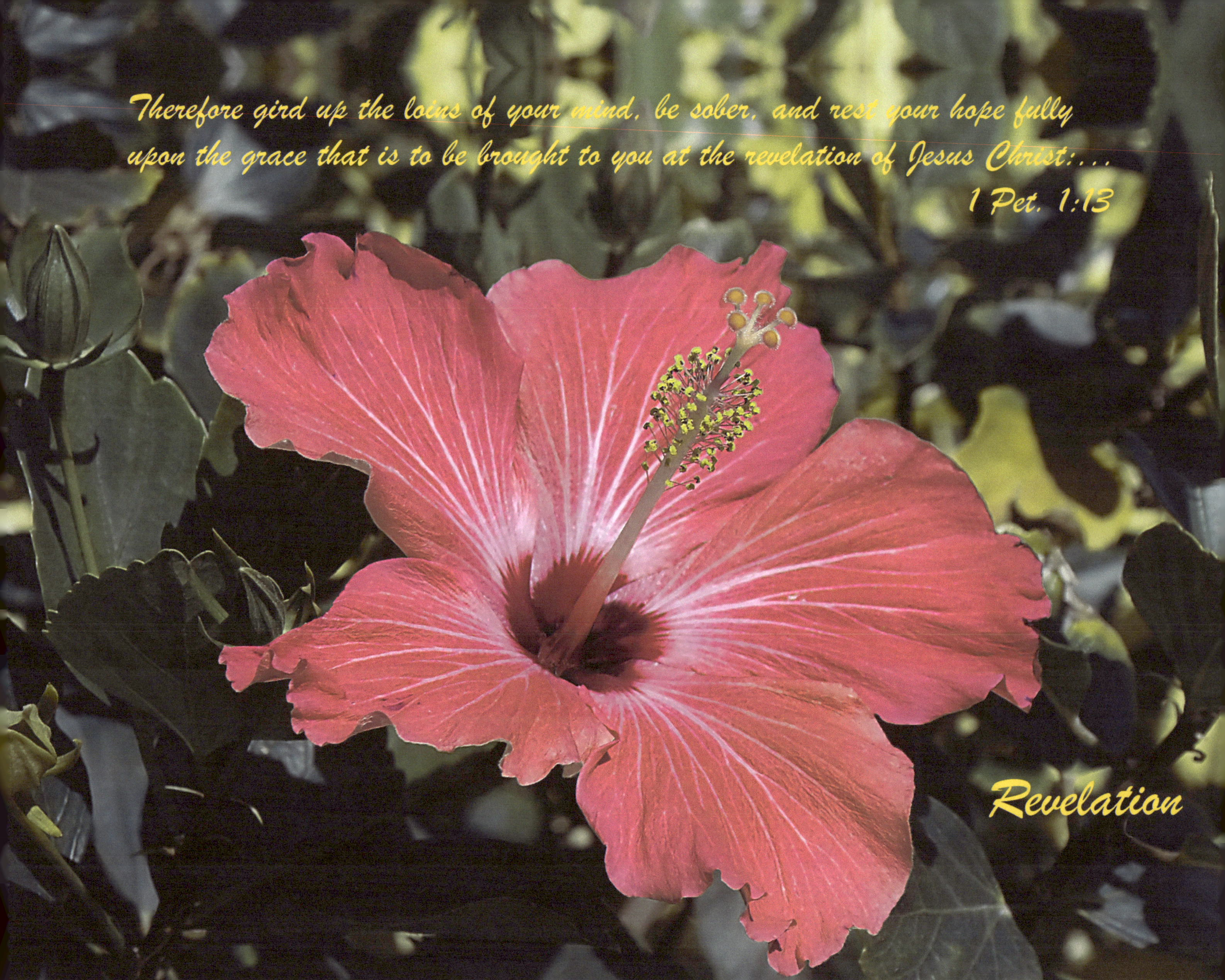
Therefore gird up the loins of your mind, be sober, and rest your hope fully
upon the grace that is to be brought to you at the revelation of Jesus Christ:...
1 Pet. 1:13
Revelation

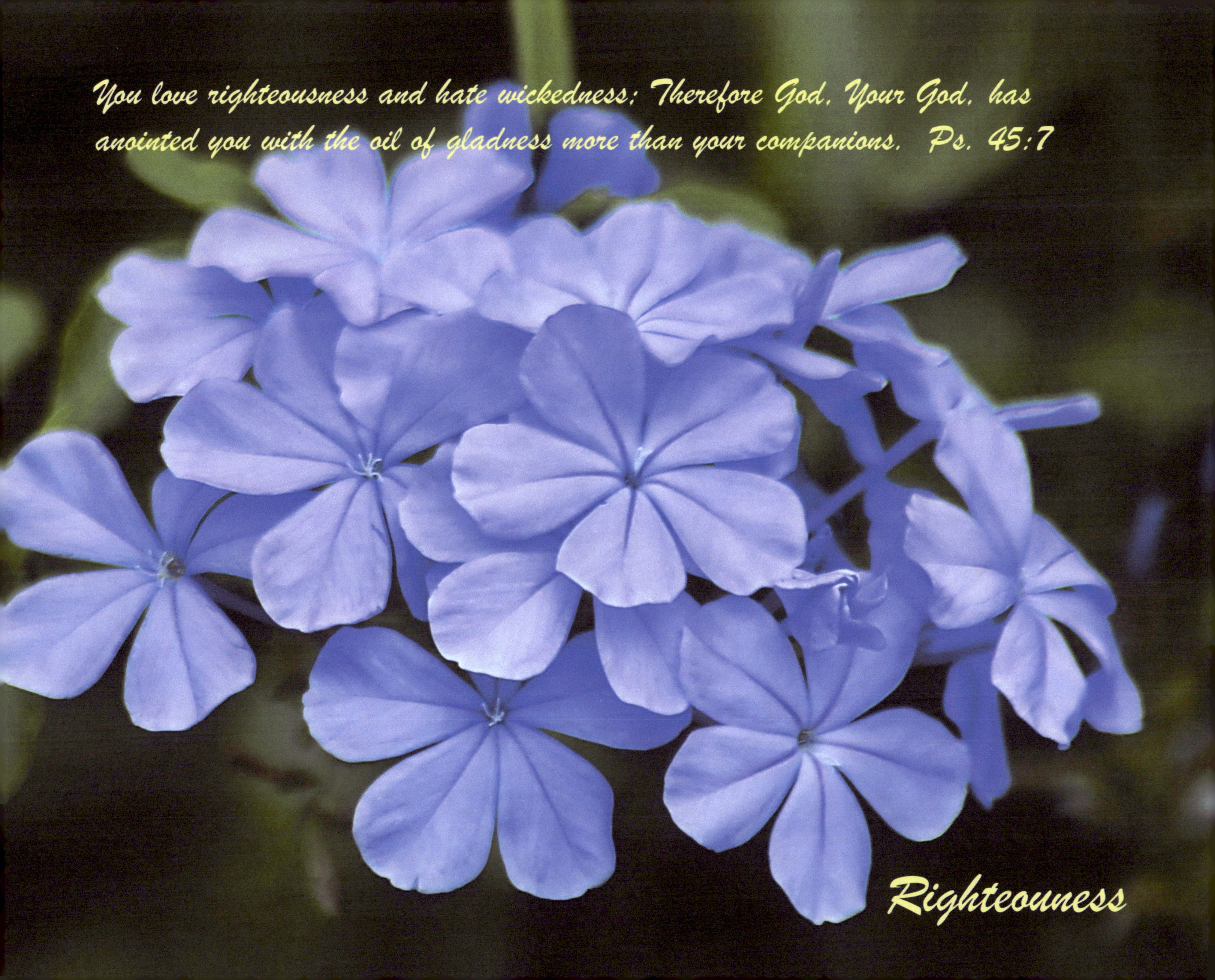

You love righteousness and hate wickedness; Therefore God, Your God, has anointed you with the oil of gladness more than your companions. Ps. 45:7

Righteouness

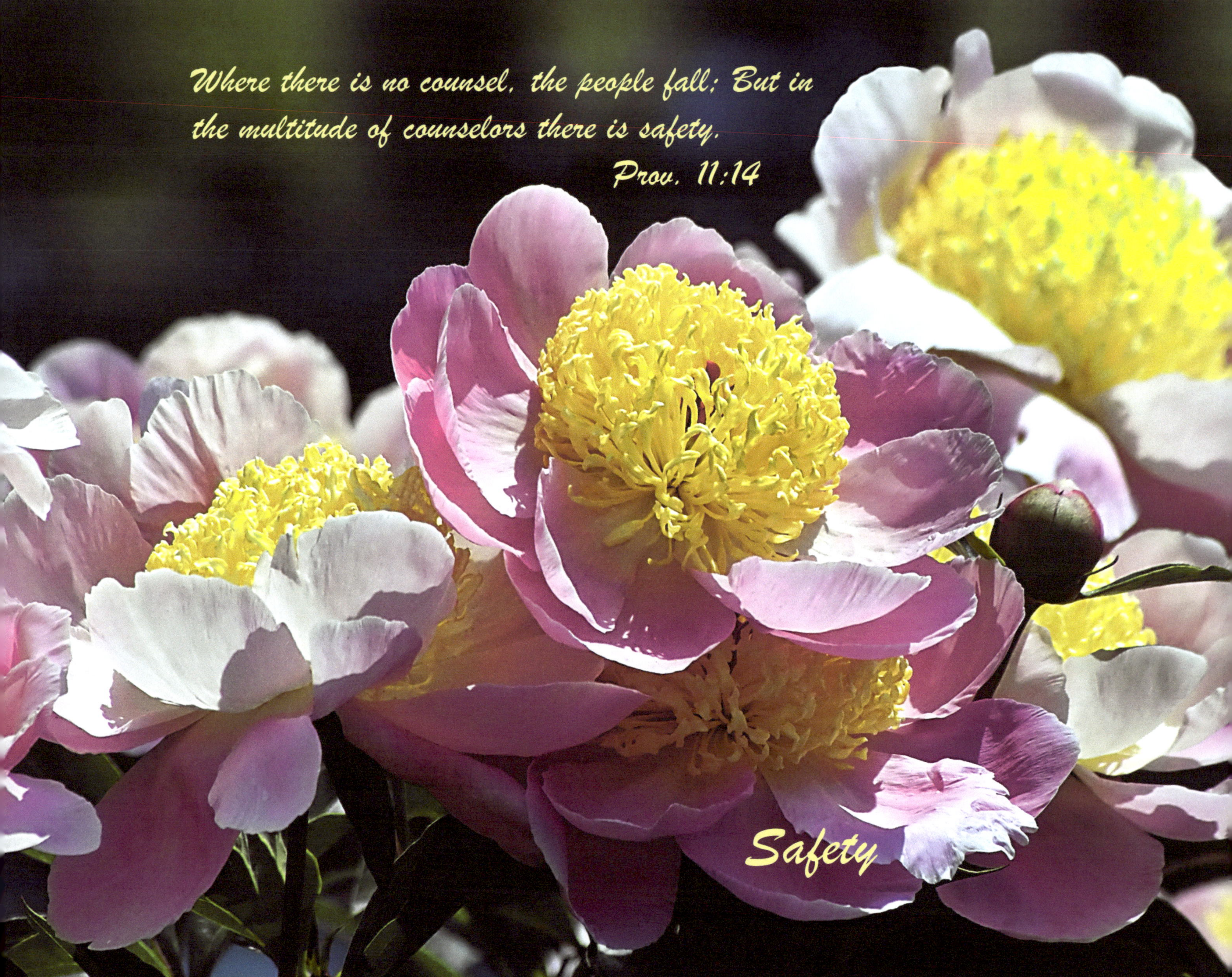
Where there is no counsel, the people fall: But in the multitude of counselors there is safety.
Prov. 11:14
Safety

For I am not ashamed of the gospel of Christ, for it is the power of God to salvation for everone who believes, for the Jew first and also for the Greek. Rom. 1:16

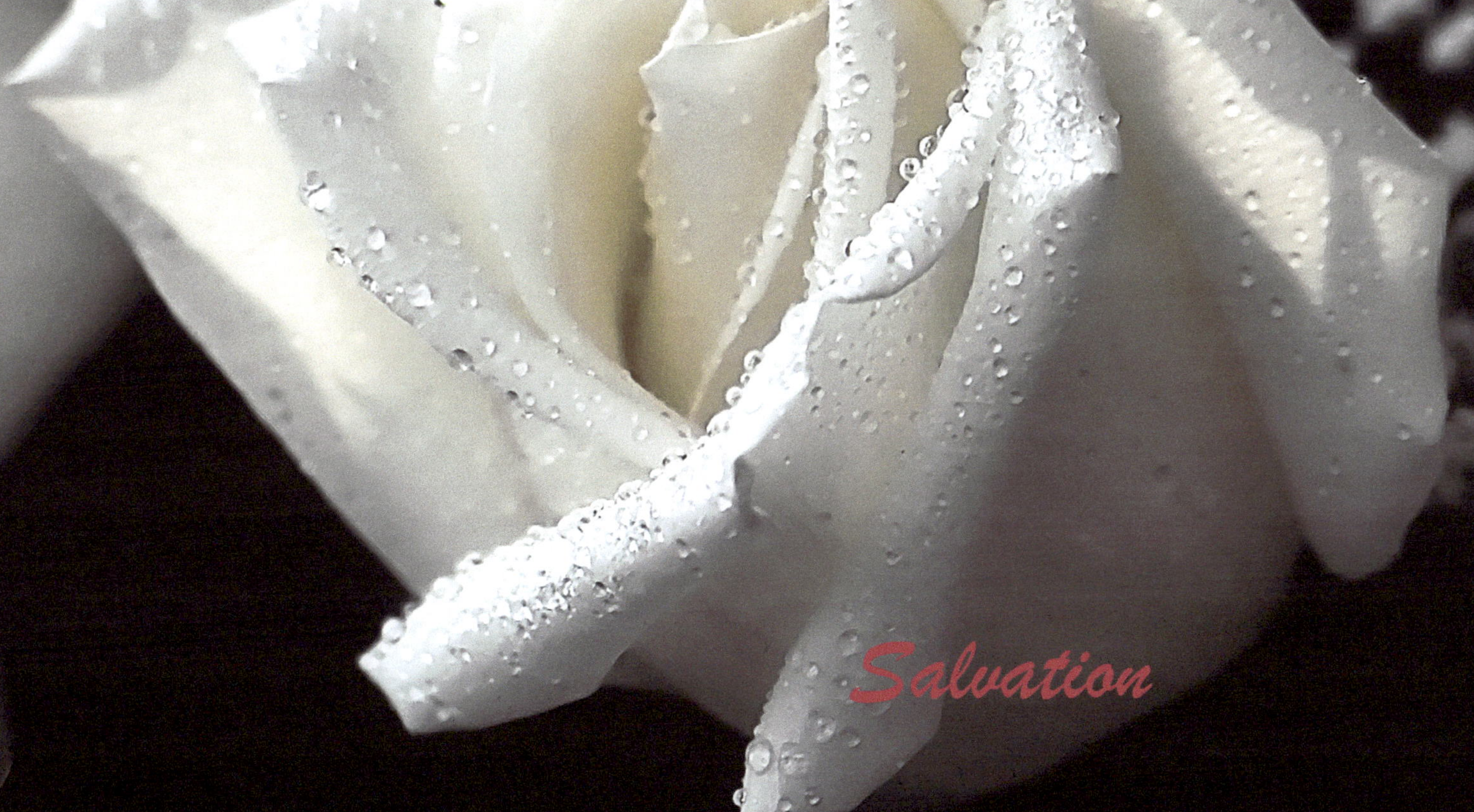

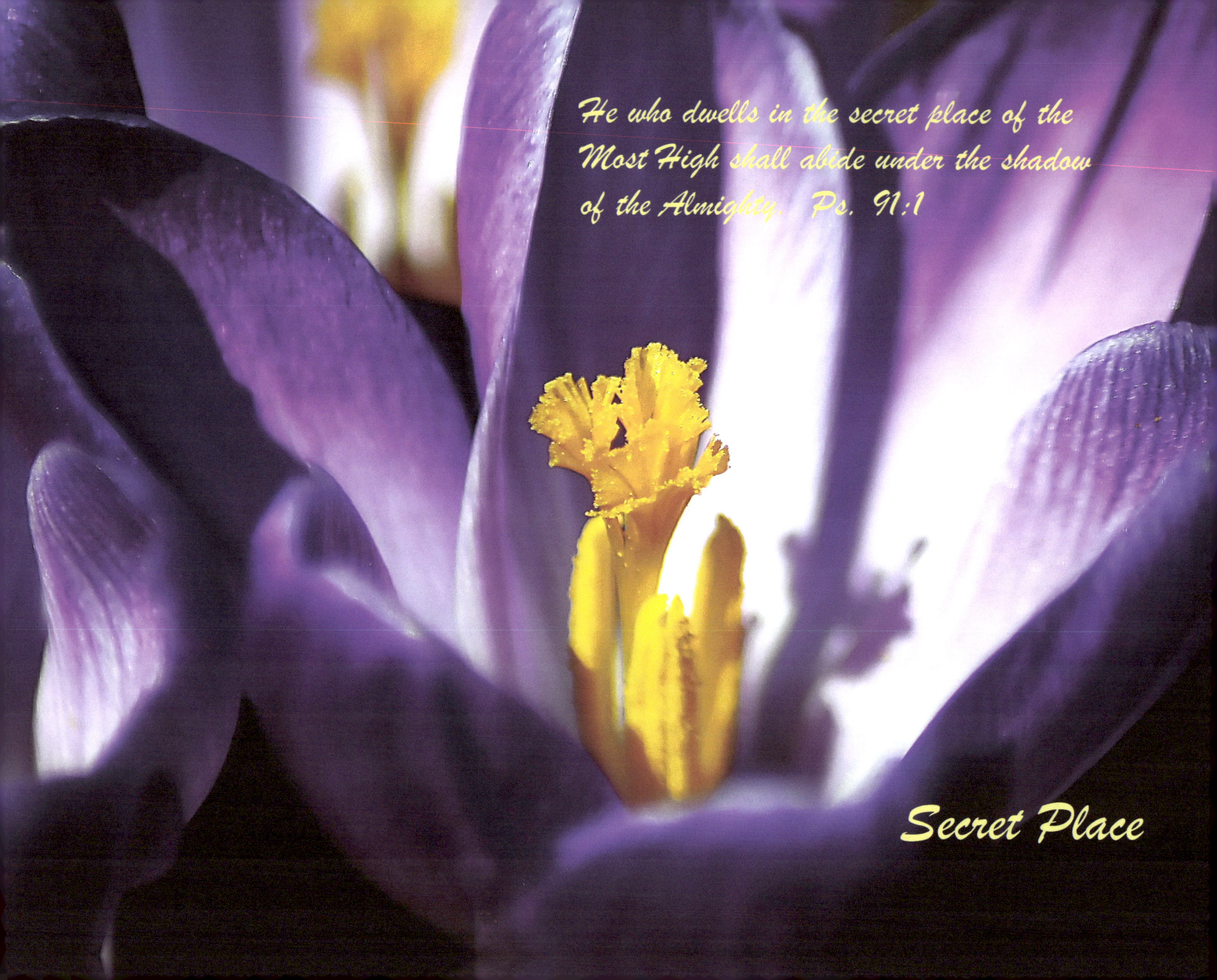

He who dwells in the secret place of the Most High shall abide under the shadow of the Almighty. Ps. 91:1

Secret Place

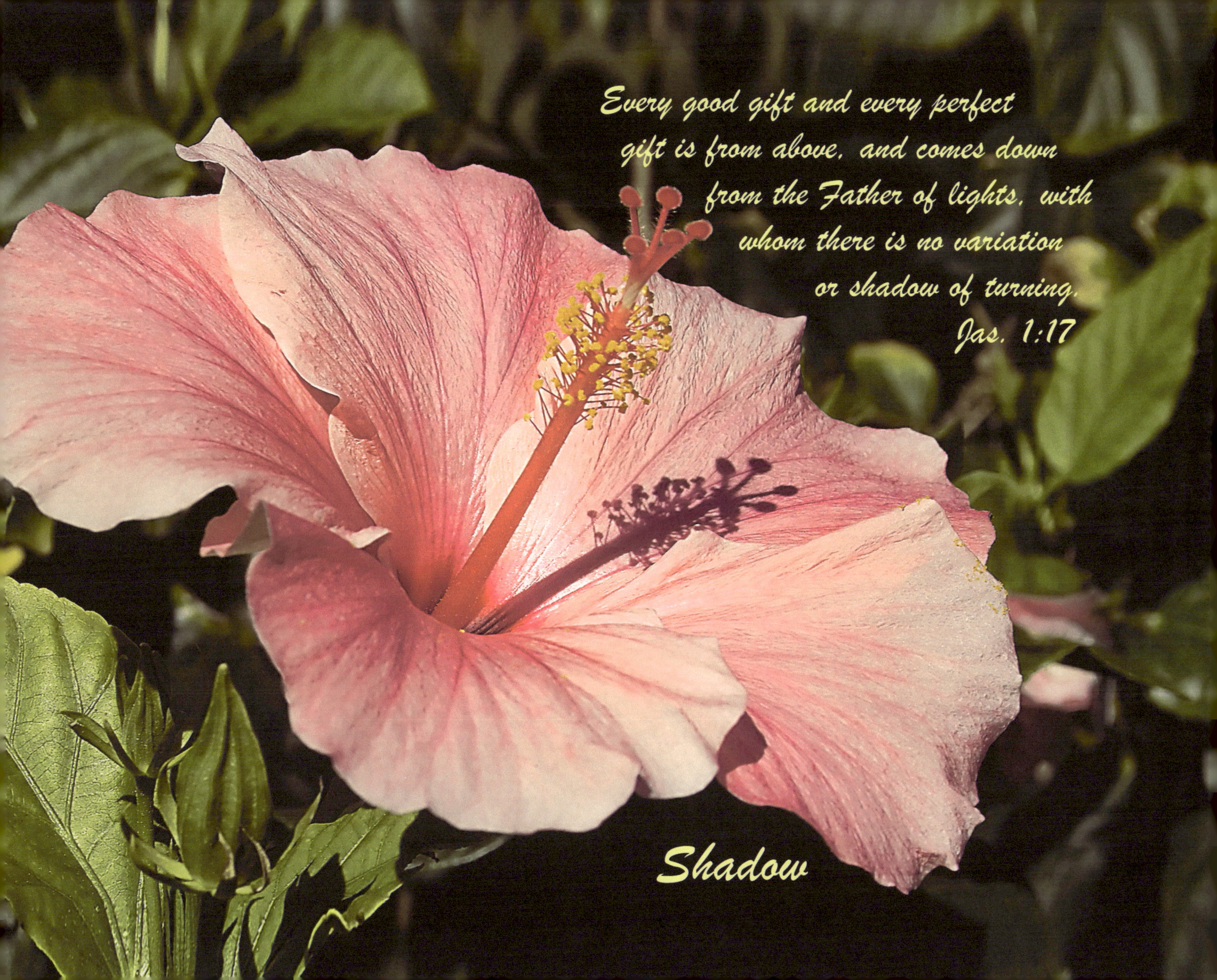

Every good gift and every perfect
gift is from above, and comes down
from the Father of lights, with
whom there is no variation
or shadow of turning.
Jas. 1:17

Shadow

... above all, taking the shield of faith with which you will be able to quench all the fiery darts of the wicked one. Eph. 6:16

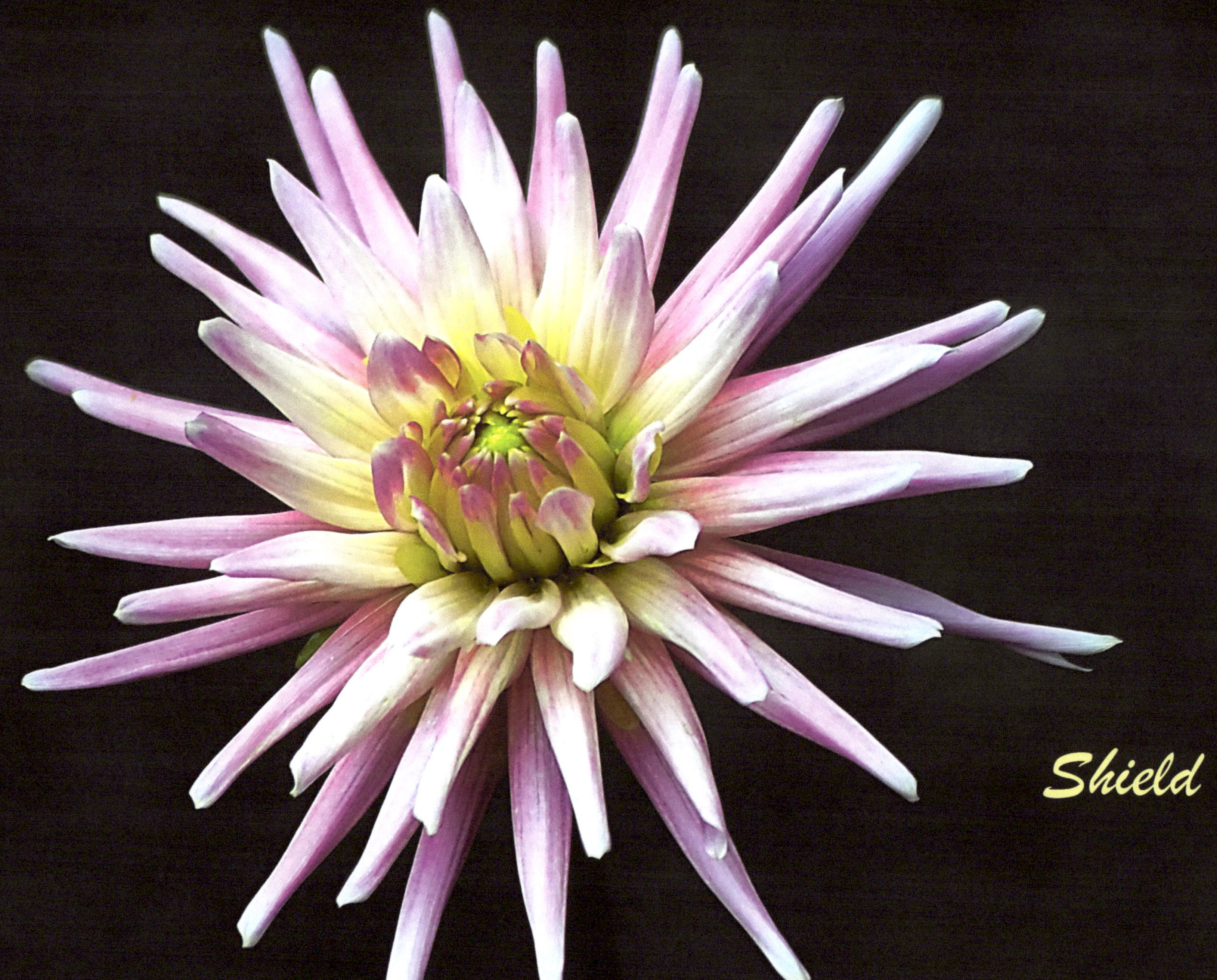

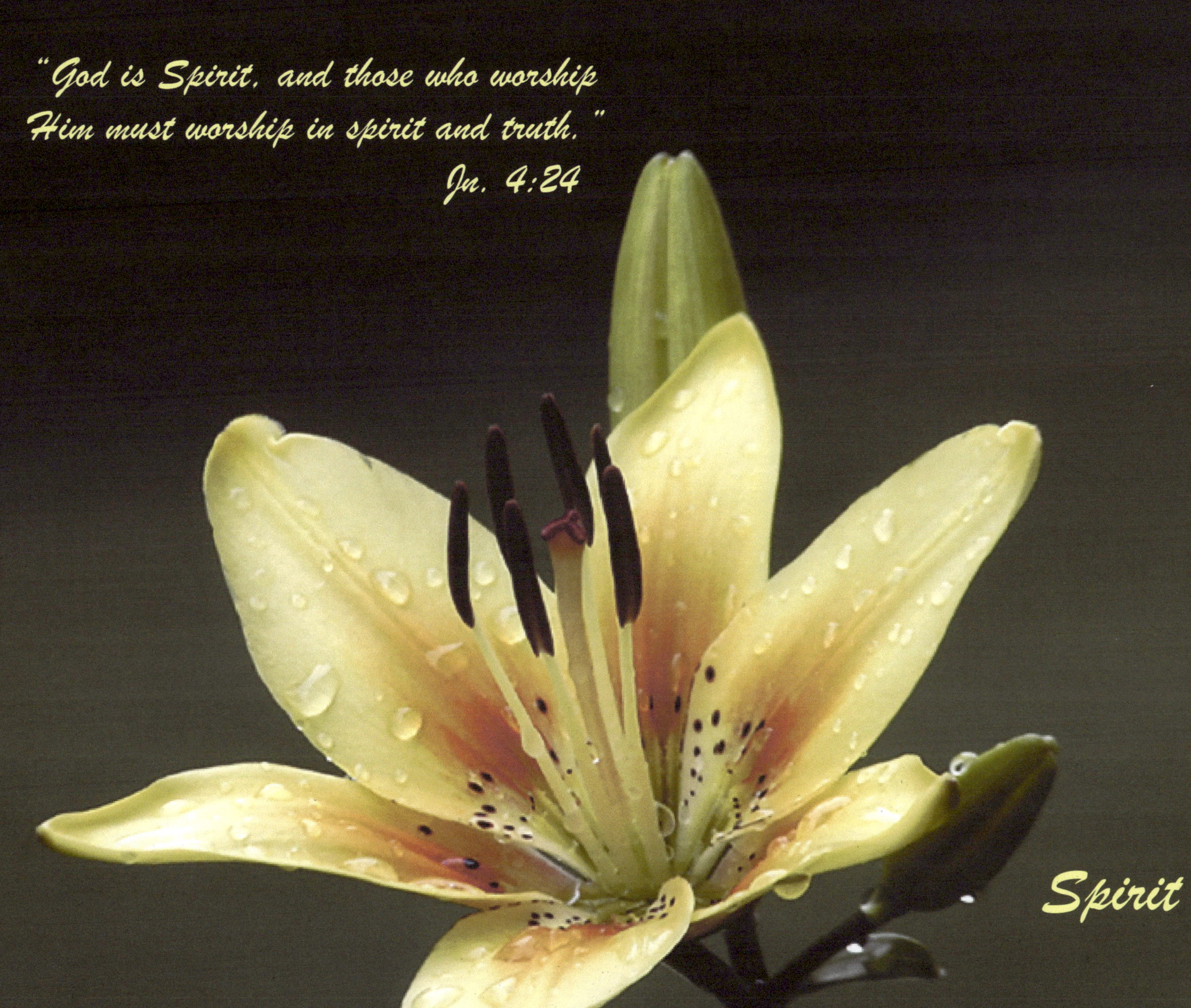
"God is Spirit, and those who worship
Him must worship in spirit and truth."
Jn. 4:24
Spirit

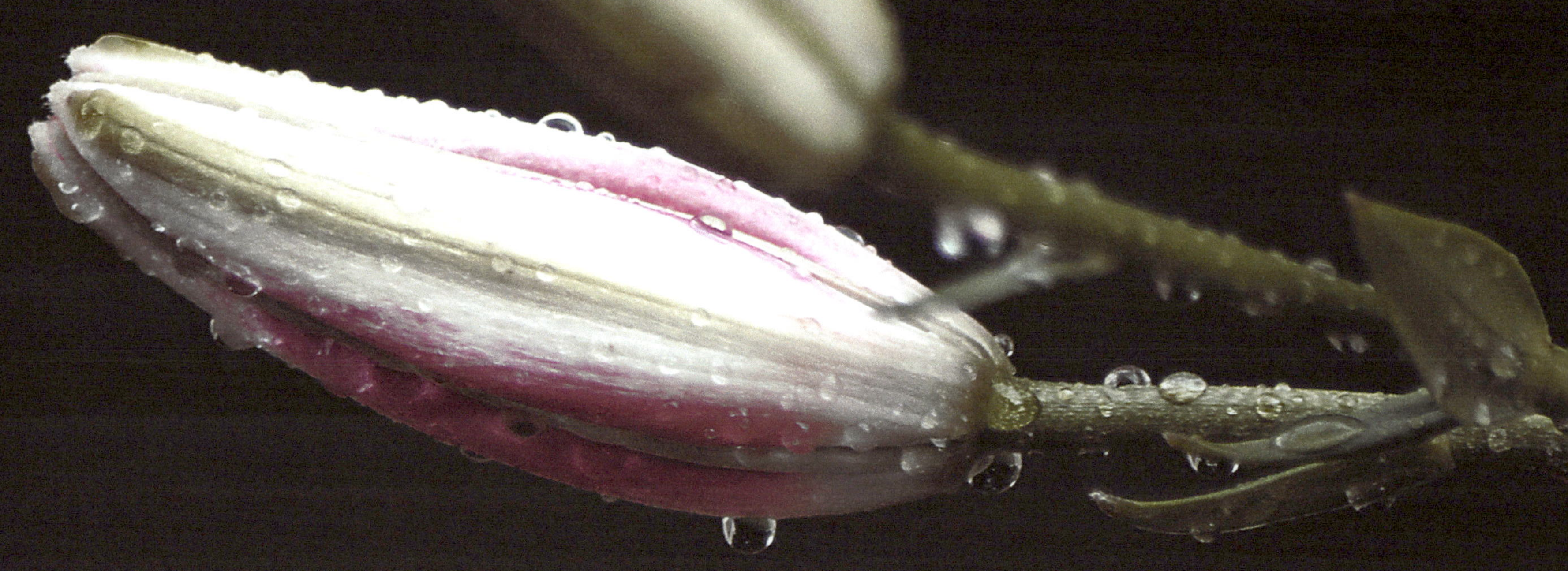
Be anxious for nothing, but in everything by prayer and
supplication, with thanksgiving, let
your requests be made known
to God. Phil. 4:6
Supplication

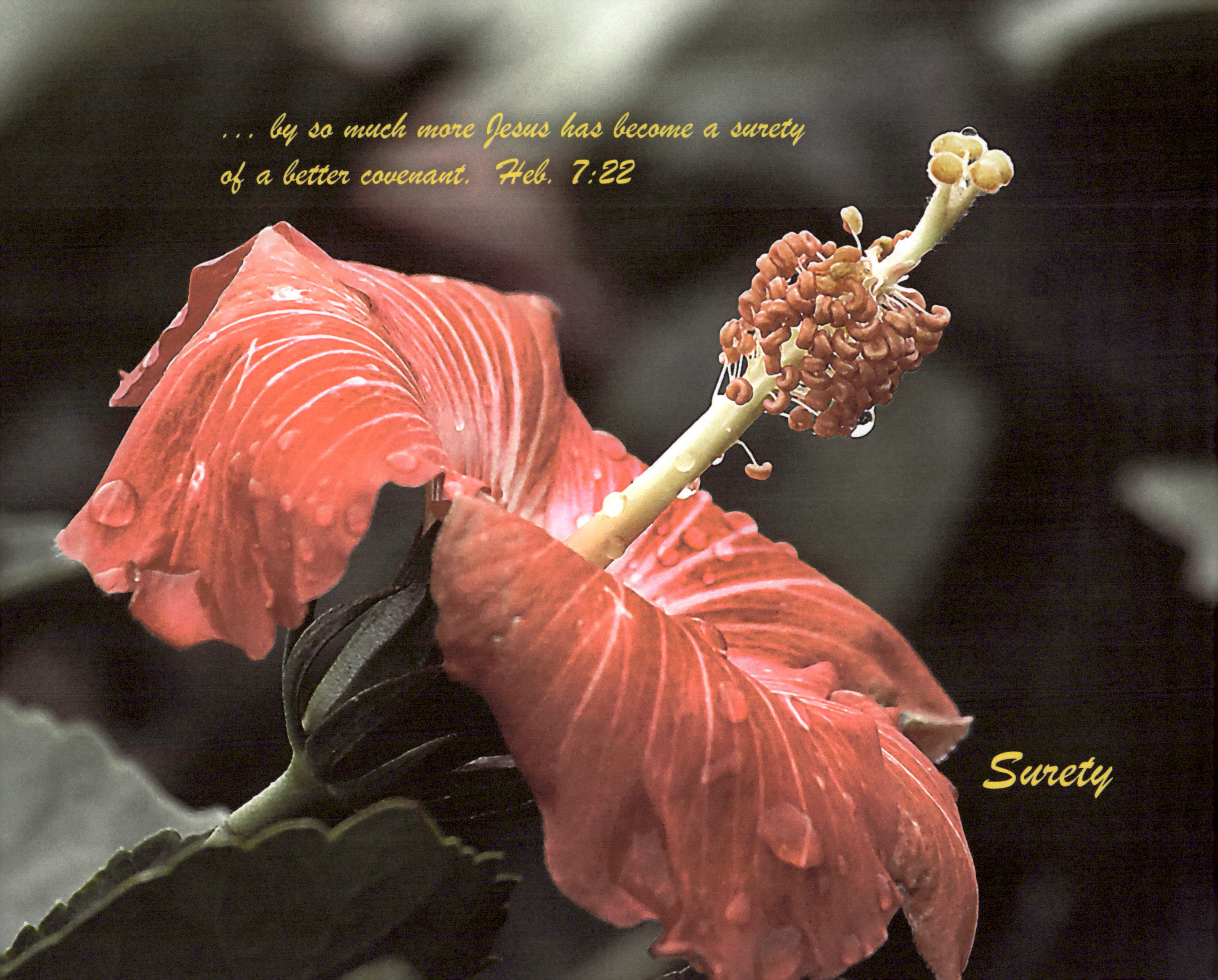
… by so much more Jesus has become a surety
of a better covenant. Heb. 7:22
Surety

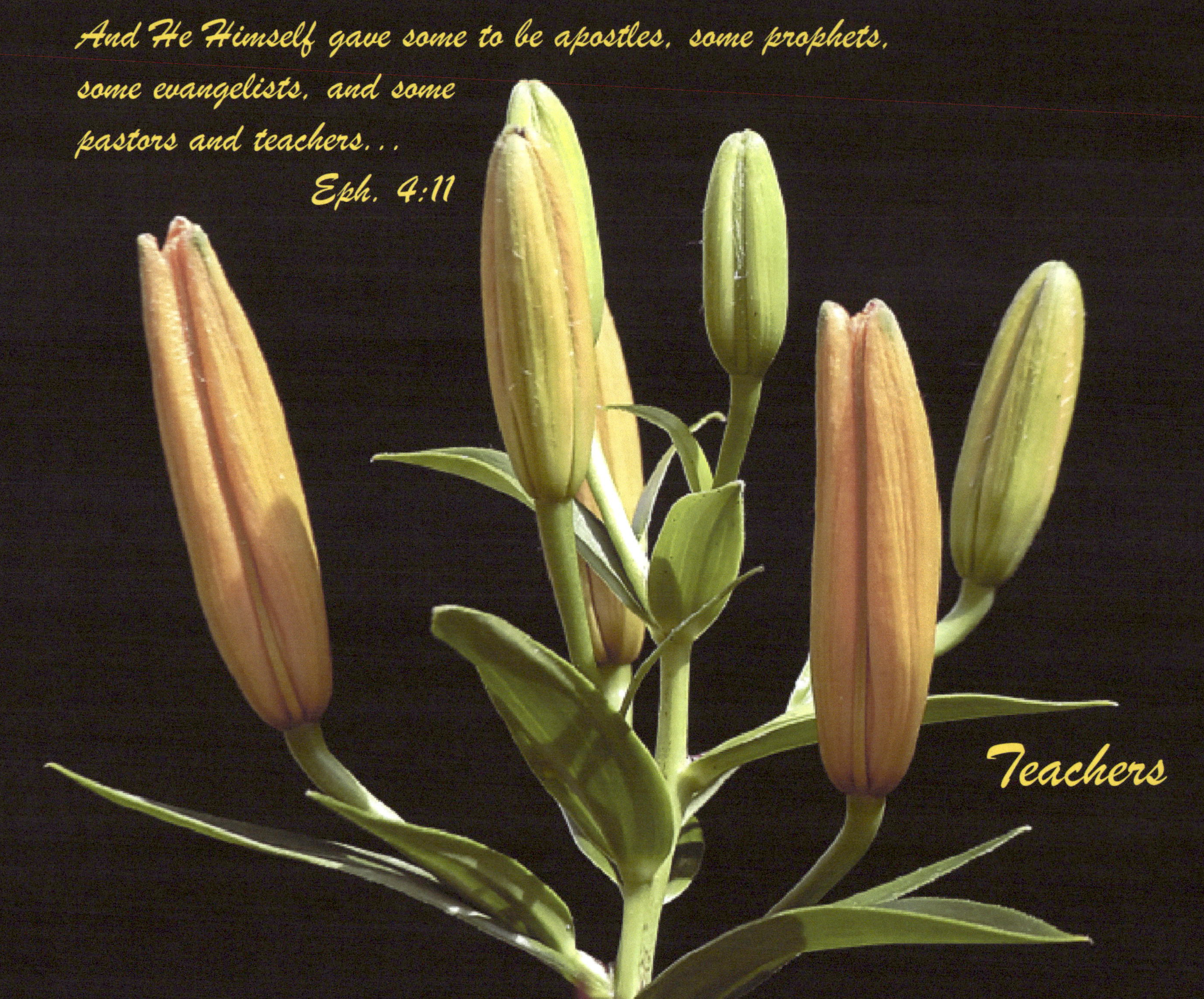
And He Himself gave some to be apostles, some prophets,
some evangelists, and some
pastors and teachers...
Eph. 4:11
Teachers

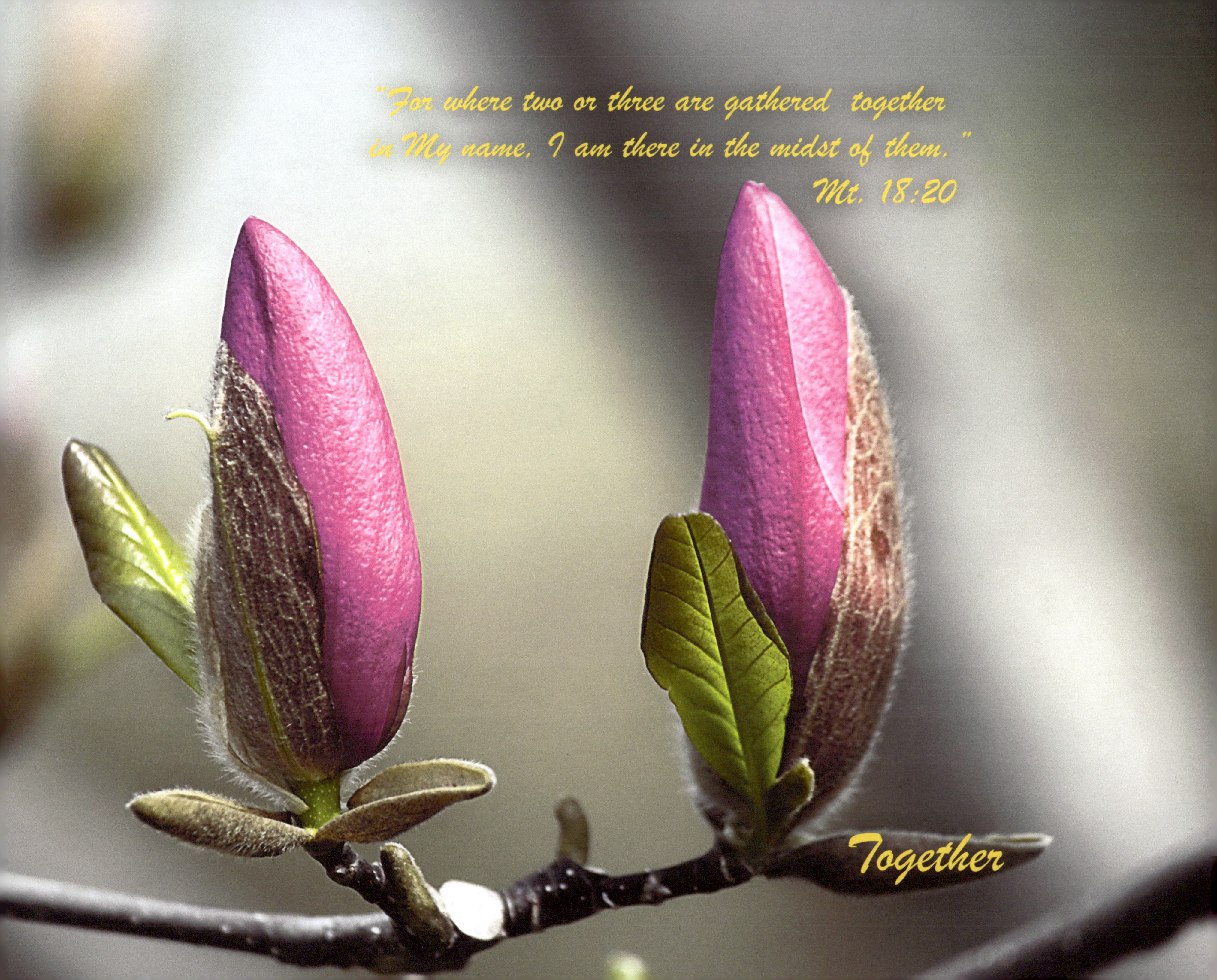

"For where two or three are gathered together
in My name, I am there in the midst of them."
Mt. 18:20

Together

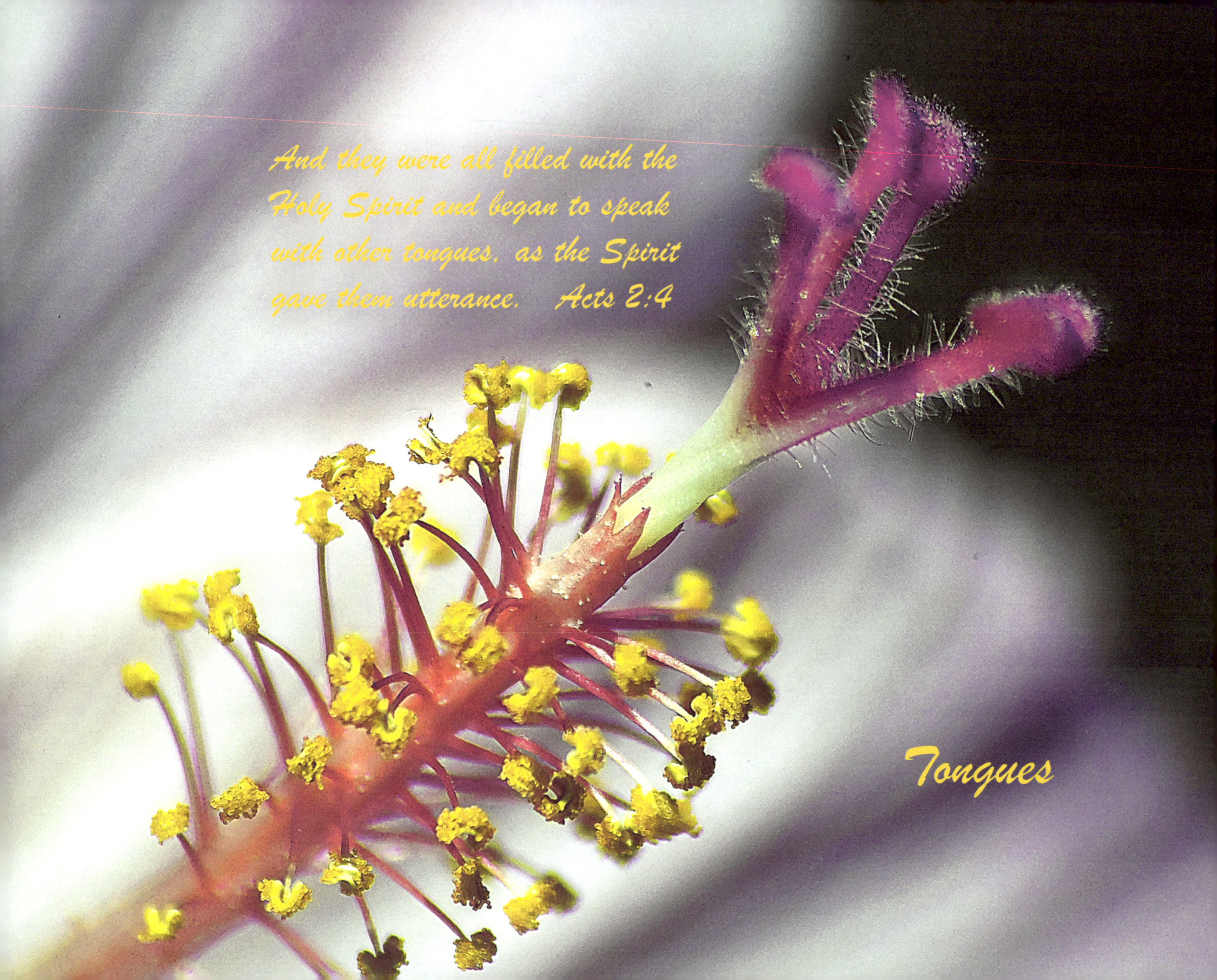

And they were all filled with the Holy Spirit and began to speak with other tongues, as the Spirit gave them utterance. *Acts 2:4*

Tongues

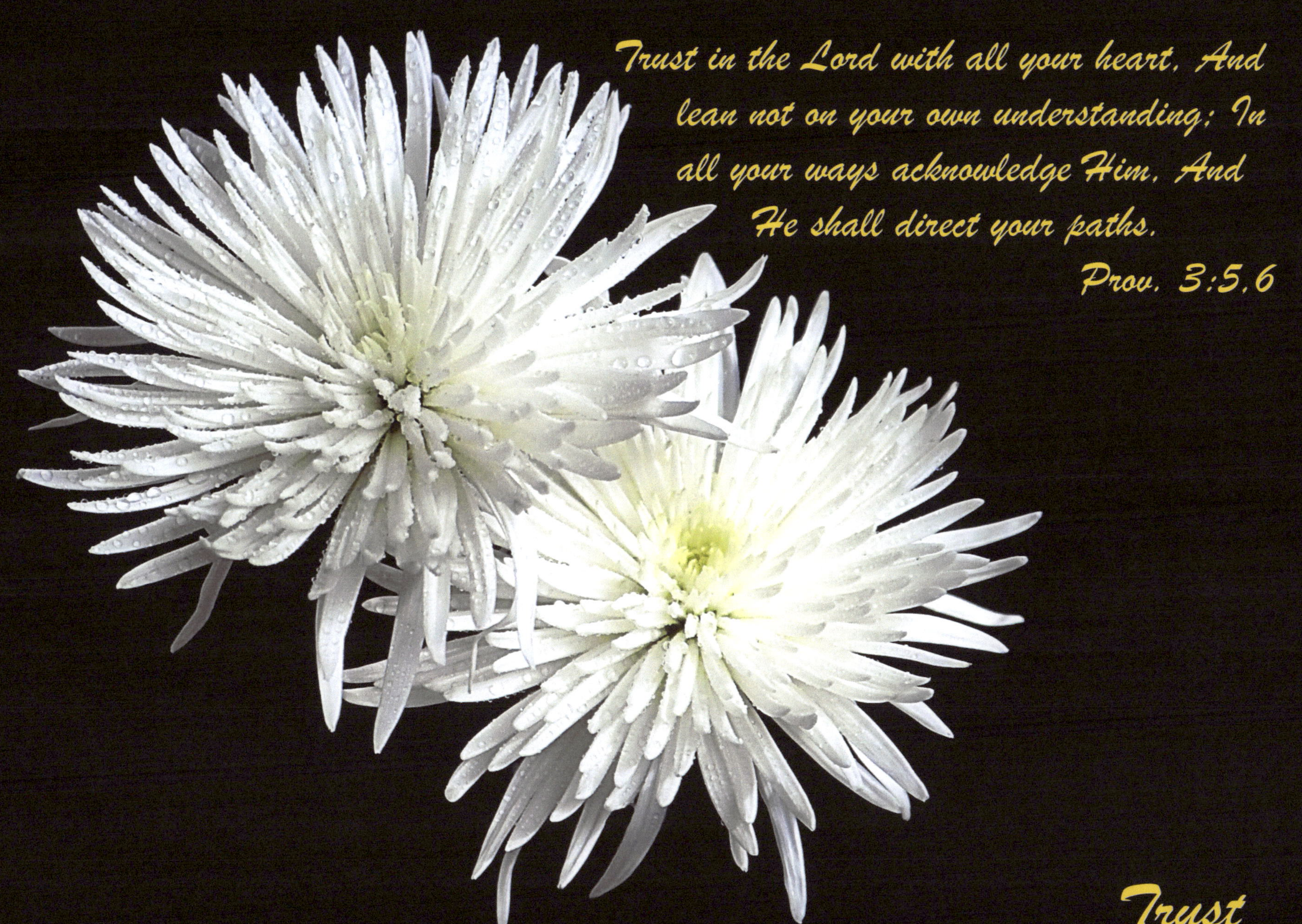
Trust in the Lord with all your heart, And
lean not on your own understanding; In
all your ways acknowledge Him, And
He shall direct your paths.
Prov. 3:5,6
Trust

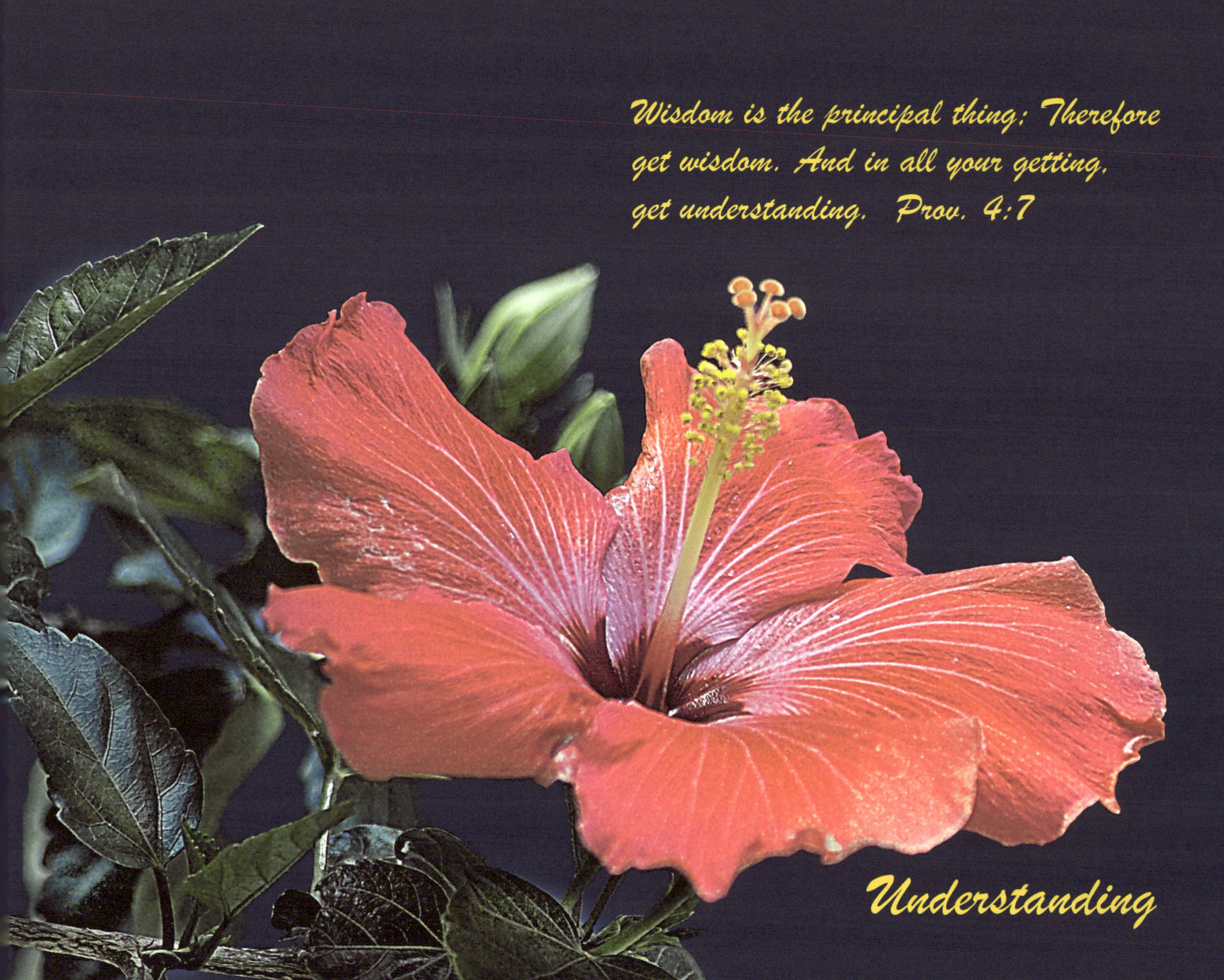
Wisdom is the principal thing: Therefore
get wisdom. And in all your getting,
get understanding. Prov. 4:7
Understanding

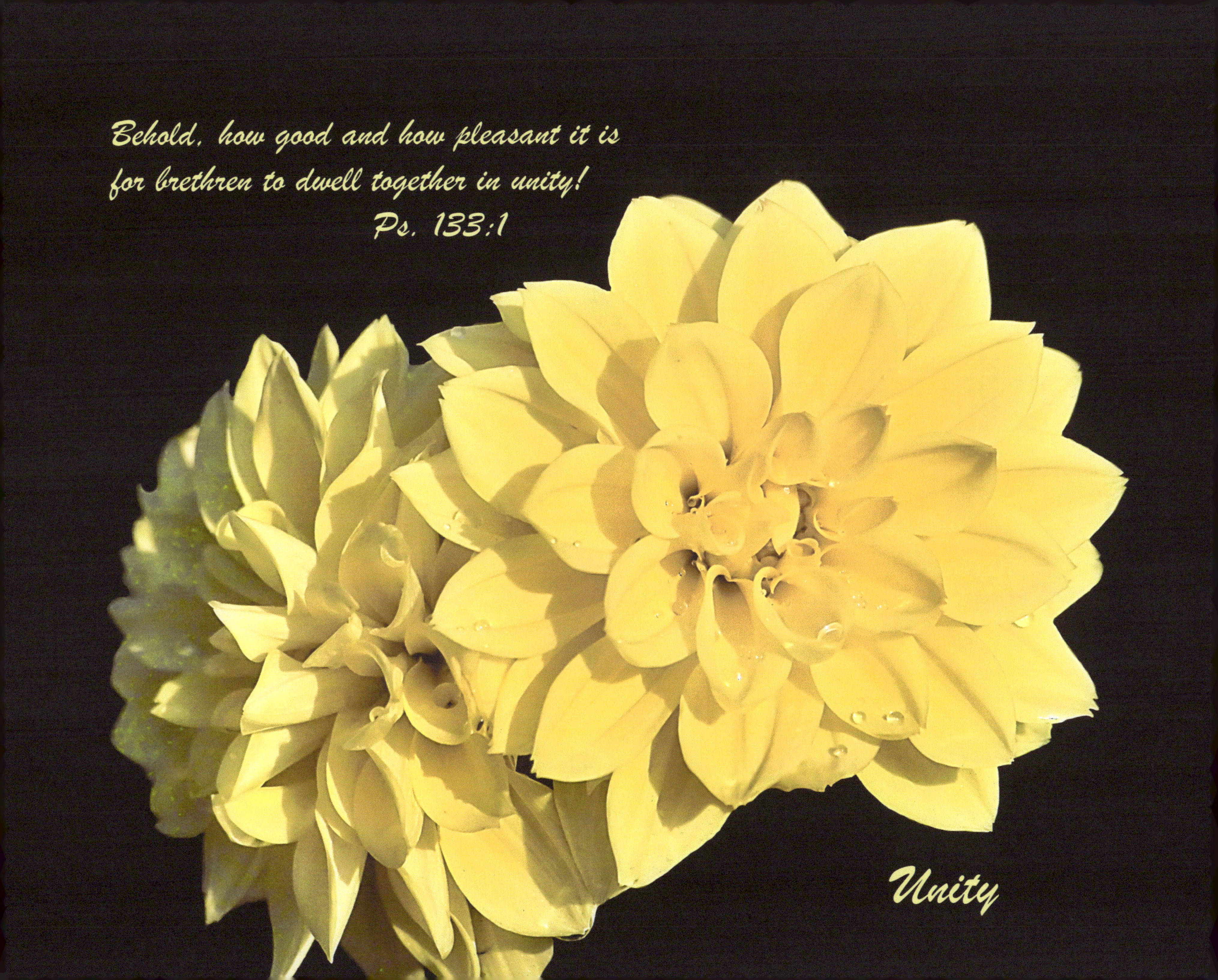

*Behold, how good and how pleasant it is
for brethren to dwell together in unity!*
Ps. 133:1

Unity

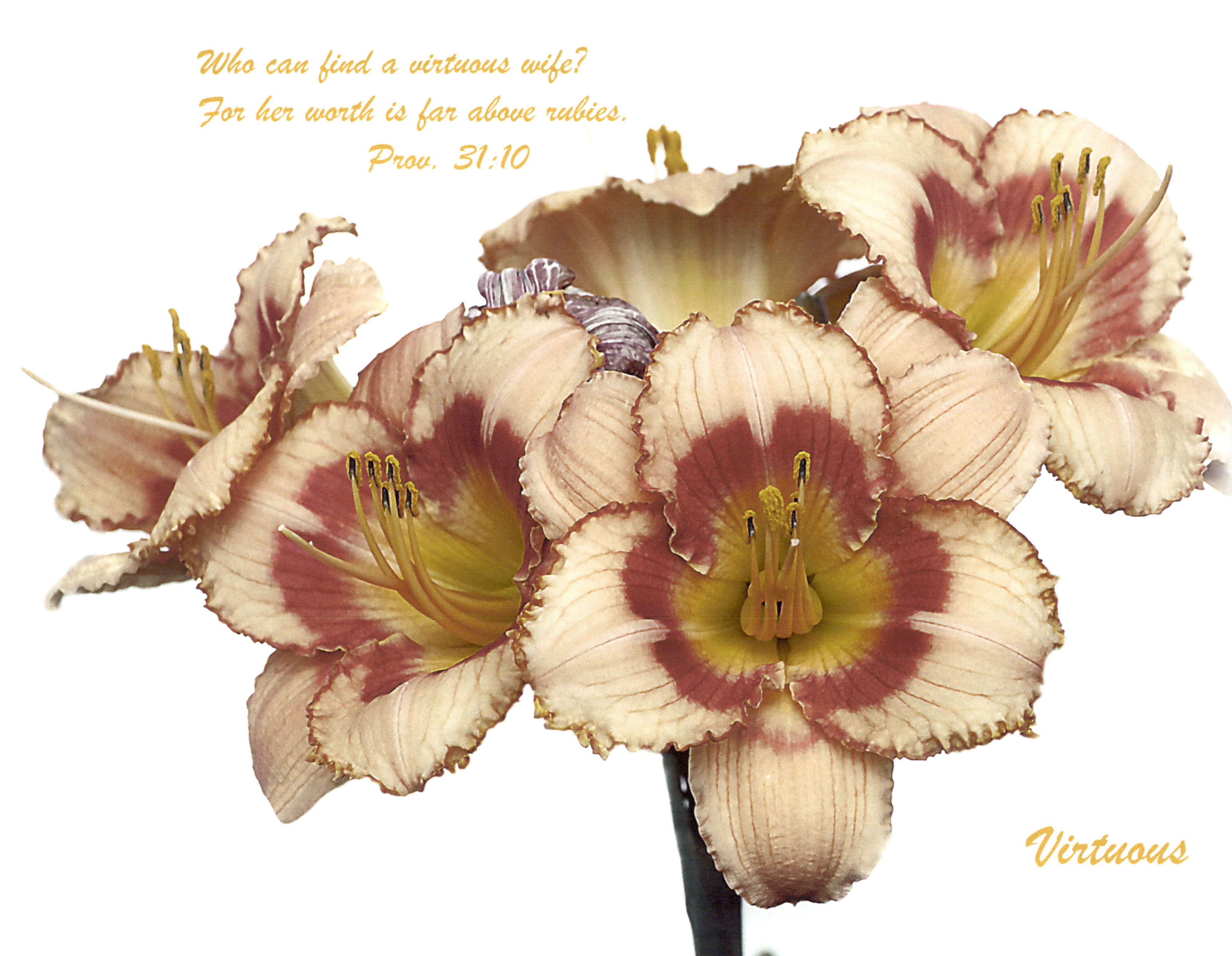

Who can find a virtuous wife?
For her worth is far above rubies.
Prov. 31:10
Virtuous

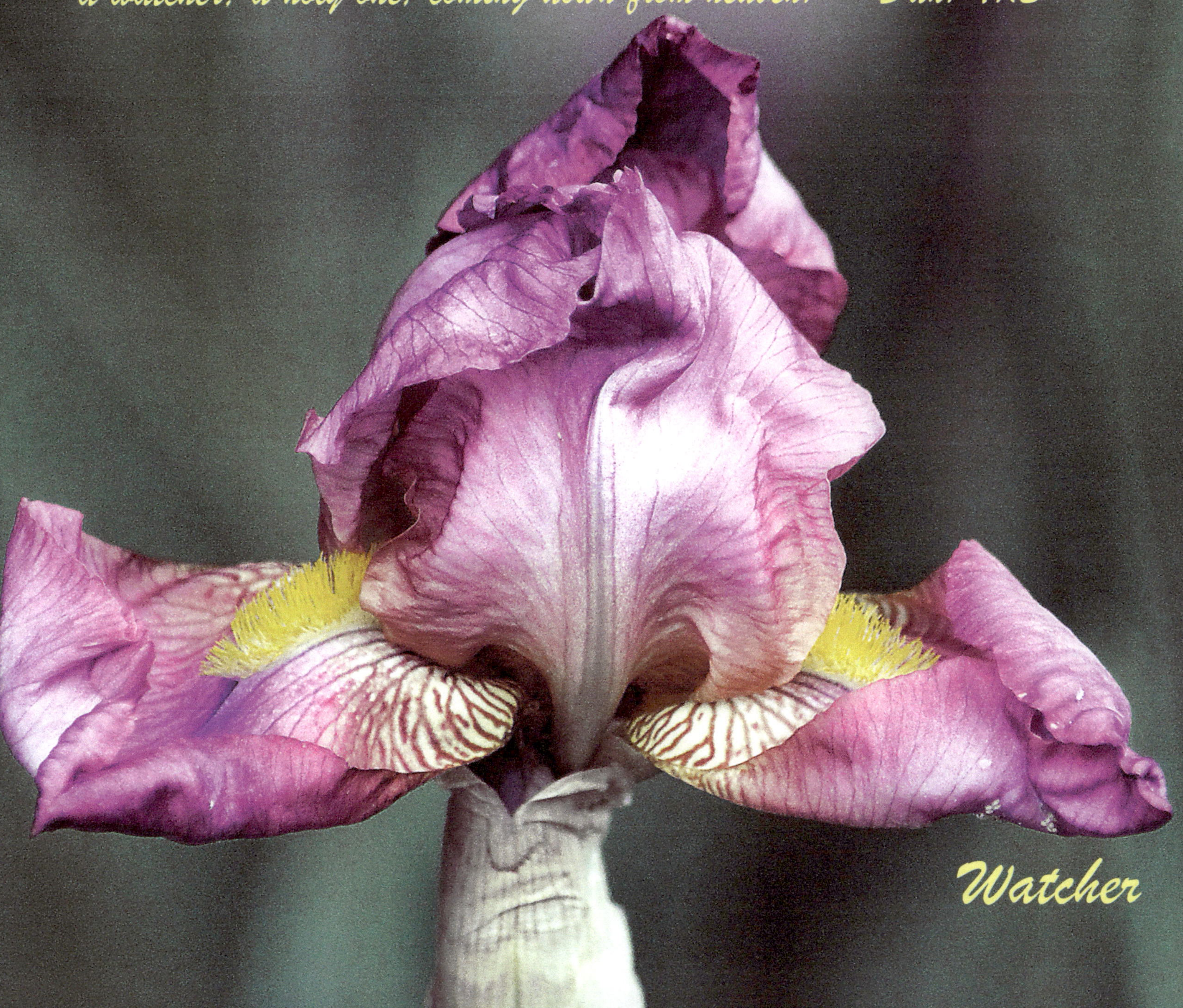
"I saw in the visions of my head while on my bed, and there was
a watcher, a holy one, coming down from heaven." Dan. 4:13
Watcher

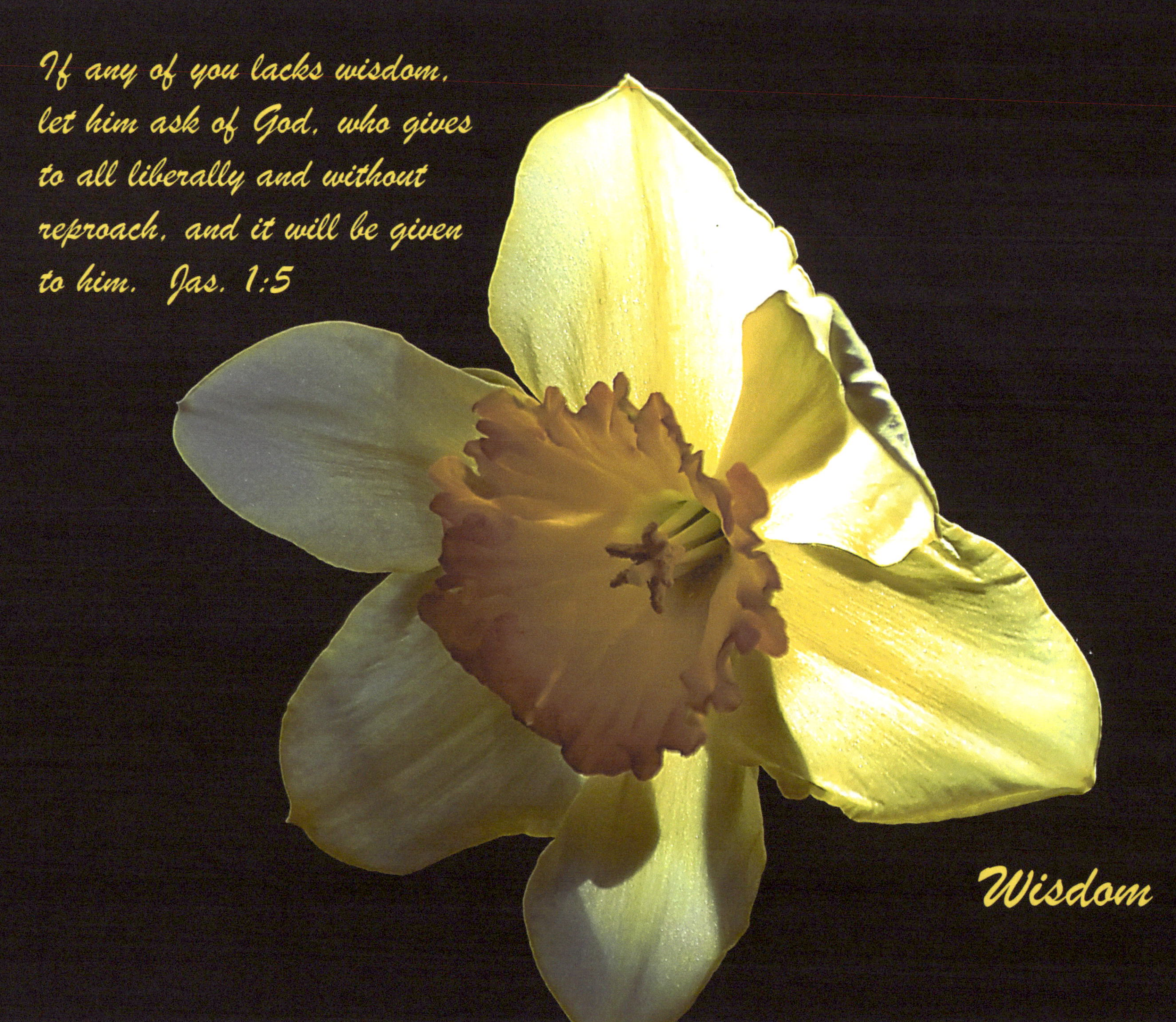
If any of you lacks wisdom,
let him ask of God, who gives
to all liberally and without
reproach, and it will be given
to him. Jas. 1:5
Wisdom

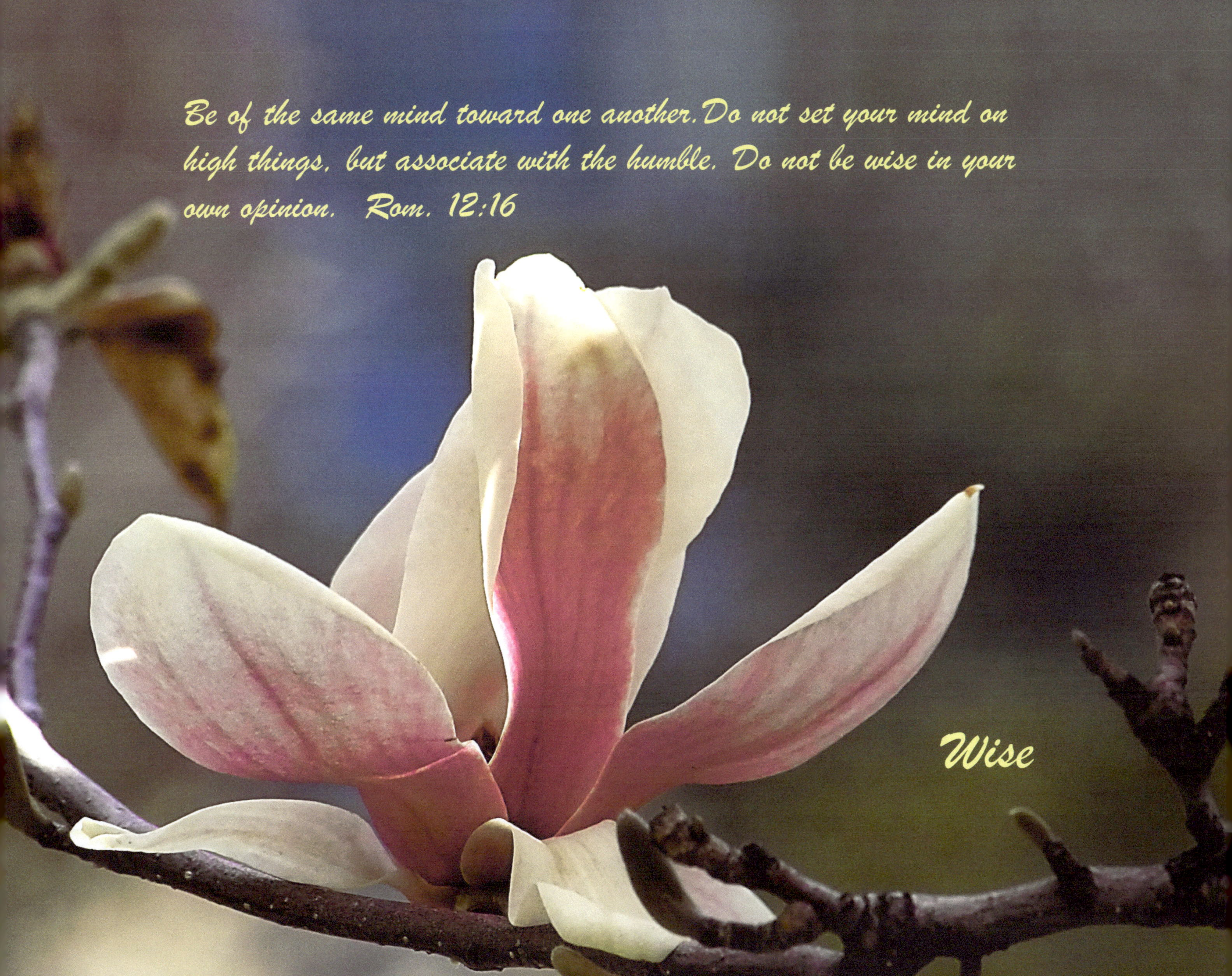
Be of the same mind toward one another.Do not set your mind on
high things, but associate with the humble. Do not be wise in your
own opinion. Rom. 12:16
Wise

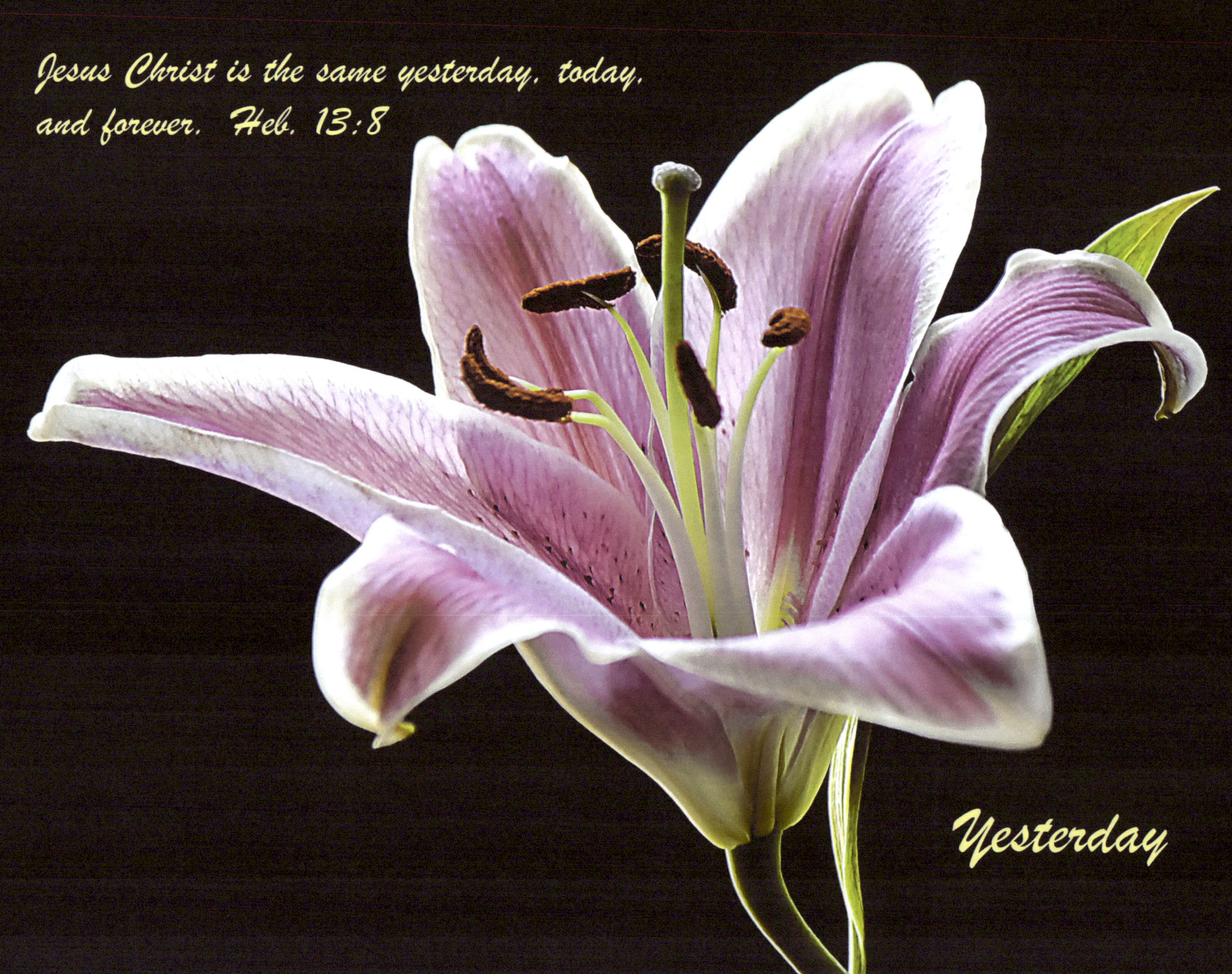
Jesus Christ is the same yesterday, today,
and forever. Heb. 13:8
Yesterday

The Lord shall go forth like a mighty man: He shall stir up His zeal like a man of war. He shall cry out, yes, shout aloud: He shall prevail against His enemies.

Is. 42:13

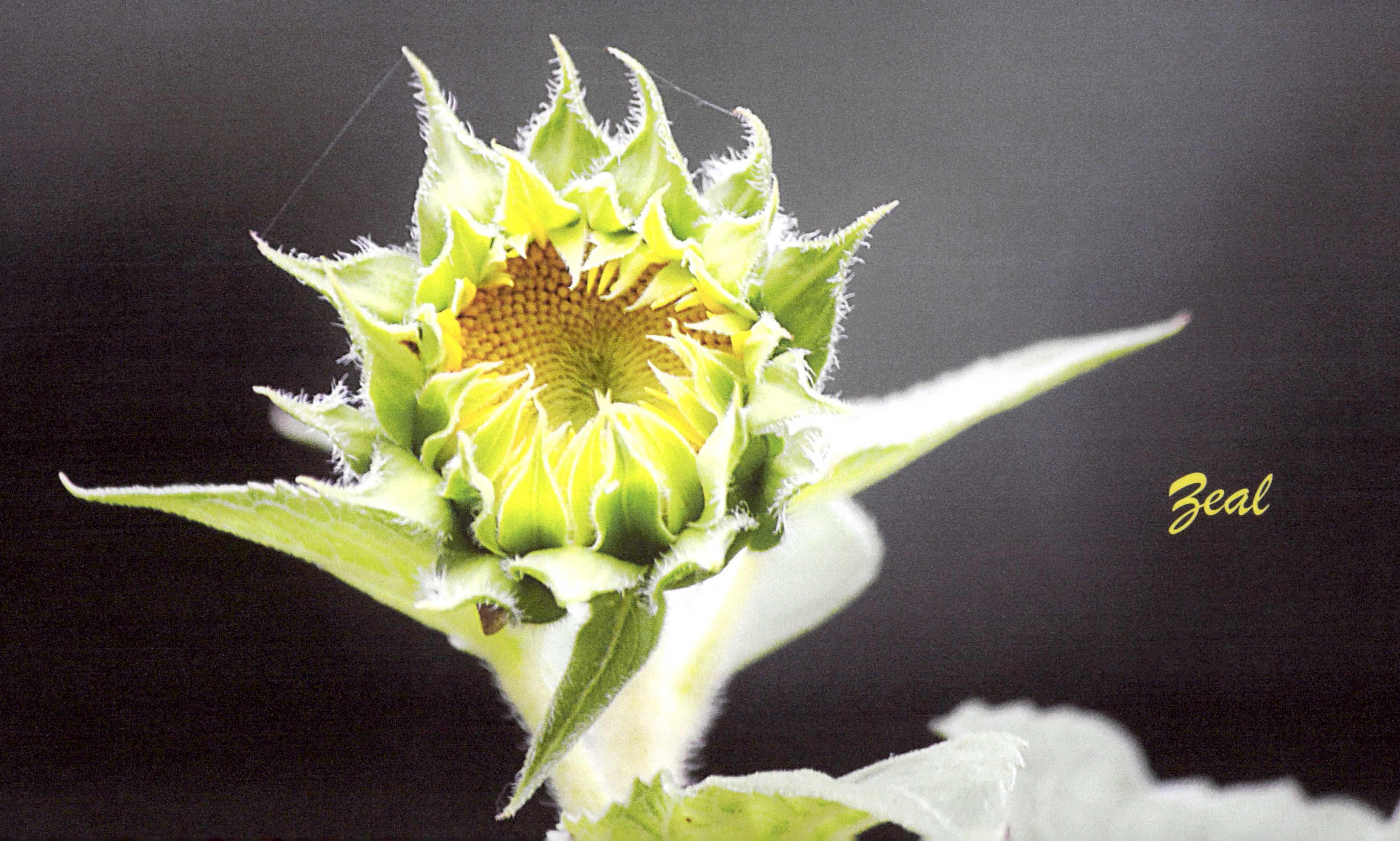

About the Photographer

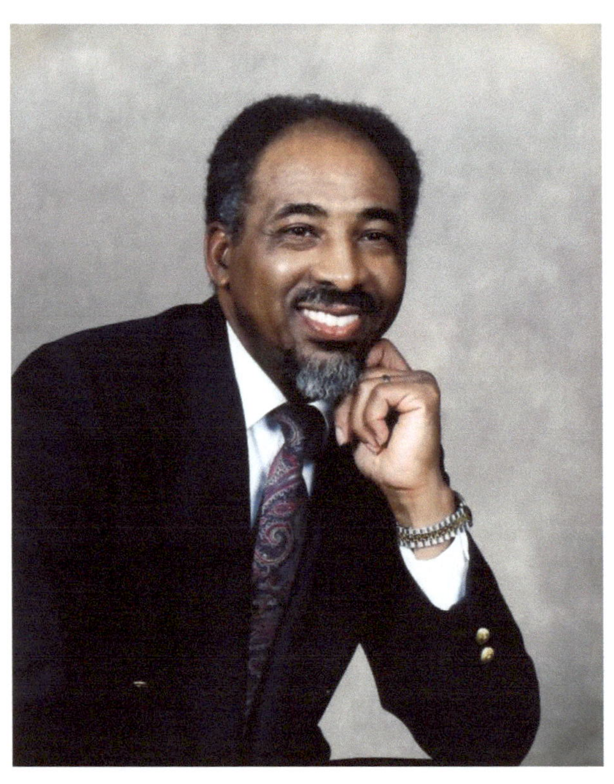

Rudolph Valentino Wiggins, Rudy to his friends and acquaintances, is a native of Norfol Virginia. Rudy is an experienced and gifted artist with a camera. He acquired his first 35m camera in 1958 upon graduation from college, and began photographing a variety of subject friends, plants, landscapes, insects, etc., anything that inspired him. He has maintained th love for photography since then. However, photography took a "back seat" to his profession pursuits as he prepared to become an educator.

He earned BS, MS, and Ph.D. degrees in education, and committed his life to teaching and research. A deeply spiritual person, Rudy purposed to make a difference in the lives of all young people. Everyone loves "Papa Rudy." He is a motivator, confidant, and a blessing to all who know him.

After retiring from professional endeavors in 2001, following forty-three years of productiv service in education as a teacher, researcher, professor, and administrator, Rudy found tin for his passion, "The Art of Photography." To him, his photographs are snapshots of God' majesty, images inspired by God's magnificent creation. When asked about his "new focus Rudy says,

"As a young man, I was inspired to use photography to express something inside of me. At the time, I didn't fully understand this motivation, and quite frankly, I still don't. However, after many years, and at this time in n life, I have a clearer insight on that inspiration. I believe it to be a gift from God. It enables me to see, and by His grace, capture imag of plants, flowers, and small creatures in a manner that reveals the beauty and majesty of His creation. I take pleasure in exploring ar recording the beauty of God for all to see and enjoy. When I photograph a flower, I give it a name inspired by Holy Scripture. I belie the Holy Spirit motivates my art."

Rudy is married to his lovely college sweetheart, Mary, and they have two daughters and six grandchildren. On December 26, 201 Rudy and Mary, celebrated fifty-nine years of marriage. He offers this publication of "Divine Inspiration" for all to share in the beau of God's flowers.

www.ingramcontent.com/pod-product-compliance
Lightning Source LLC
LaVergne TN
LVHW072330100826
845154LV00009B/149
9780999465387